EVERYTHING
IS SPIRITUAL

ALSO BY ROB BELL

EVERYTHING
IS SPIRITUAL

Who We Are and What We're Doing Here

ROB BELL

ST. MARTIN'S
ESSENTIALS
NEW YORK

First published in the United States by St. Martin's Essentials,
an imprint of St. Martin's Publishing Group

www.stmartins.com

Designed by Steven Seighman

Library of Congress Cataloging-in-Publication Data

Names: Bell, Rob, 1970– author.
Title: Everything is spiritual : who we are and what we're
   doing here / Rob Bell.
Description: First edition. | New York : St. Martin's Essentials, 2020.
Identifiers: LCCN 2020019315 | ISBN 9781250620569 (hardcover) |
   ISBN 9781250781710 (international, sold outside the U.S., subject to
   rights availability) | ISBN 9781250620576 (ebook)
Subjects: LCSH: Bell, Rob, 1970– | Religion and science. | Spirituality. |
   Theological Anthropology. | Philosophical theology.
Classification: LCC BL73.B45 A3 2020 | DDC 204—dc23
LC record available at https://lccn.loc.gov/2020019315

Our books may be purchased in bulk for promotional, educational,
or business use. Please contact your local bookseller or the Macmillan
Corporate and Premium Sales Department at 1-800-221-7945, extension
5442, or by email at MacmillanSpecialMarkets@macmillan.com.

First U.S. Edition: 2020
First International Edition: 2020

10 9 8 7 6 5 4 3 2 1

Think of the big moves you have already made, from a single cell to a human being. Stay light-footed, and keep moving.

—Rumi

EVERYTHING IS SPIRITUAL

My grandma kept cash in her bra.
I'd ask her for a twenty, and she'd reach in there, pull out a wad, and say,
Will a ten and two fives do?

When I was in high school in the mid-'80s I used to visit her on her farm. We lived in Okemos, a suburb of Lansing, the state capital in the center of Michigan. I'd drive our Oldsmobile out into the country to her old brick farmhouse, which was surrounded by barns and pastures and fields. I'd park in the driveway and then her dog, Gunner, would circle the car, peeing on all four tires. She'd often make dinner, and then afterward we'd sit on her porch in white wicker chairs.

I remember the wind, how it would blow across the fields and in among the barns and move the chimes hanging from the eaves on that porch. Sometimes we'd talk, other times we'd sit for long periods in silence. I was in that tenuous space between being a boy and being a man, trying to sort out who I was and where I was headed, surrounded by all the dramas and insanities of high school.

Everything around me was ranked. There were the best students and the best athletes and the coolest kids who got invited to all the right parties. Everywhere I turned there was someone better. Someone smarter, faster, more tuned in to those ambiguous codes that sort out who gets it and who doesn't. I lived with this perpetual ache that I was a half step behind, haunted by those questions:

Do I have what it takes?
Will I ever find my place?
Am I good enough?

But then I'd sit there in one of those wicker chairs and those questions would temporarily fade away, and I'd listen to that wind, and in those moments in that place everything was all right even if it wasn't.

I experienced a wordlessness there on that porch, a sublime state of grace in which the presence of another communicates a world of truth without any sentences or statements.

Sometimes my grandma would tell me about the great love of her life, her first husband, Preston, my dad's father. Preston served on an aircraft carrier in the Pacific Ocean in World War II. The day he came home from the war he walked in the house, greeted his family, dropped off his bags, and then left the house to find a job, which he went to first thing the next morning. The stories she told about Preston were like that one—full of action and purpose. This wasn't a man who sat around waiting for things to happen. He'd gotten cancer during the war, and he died when he was thirty-four.

According to my dad no one told him and his brother, Douglas, about the seriousness of their dad's illness. One day my dad's uncle came by and told him he had to take him somewhere. My dad got in the back seat of his uncle's car, saw his cousin sitting there, and asked,
Where are we going?

His cousin replied,
Your dad died. We're going to the funeral home.

When they arrived at the funeral home, my dad was told that he wasn't allowed to cry because they were happy that his dad was now in heaven.

My dad was eight at the time, his brother, Douglas, was six.

When my dad was seventeen, he and his brother were involved in an accident. Douglas was critically injured, and an ambulance came to get him. My grandma got in the ambulance with him as it left for the hospital, leaving my dad at the scene. The next morning he learned that his brother had died, and then at the funeral he was told,
You aren't going to shed any tears, because we're happy that Douglas is in heaven.

My grandma's name was Eileen,
my dad's name is Rob,
and from an early age I could feel the history between them.
Love, yes.

Loyalty, absolutely.
But also a certain lingering melancholy, a muted grief
hovering in the air between them. They didn't come from
a culture where you talk about your pain, the dominant
messages they picked up were more along the lines of
Be good
Keep moving
Follow the rules
and
Trust that this is all some sort of divine plan.

So they did.

They'd experienced unspeakable loss, together, and it had
bonded them to each other, but it was a bond forever tinged
with loss.

I picked up on all that muted grief floating in the air
between my grandma and dad, and from an early age I just
wanted to make them laugh.

That's what I remember.
I made her laugh.
I made him laugh.
If I could get them laughing so hard they were in tears,
I knew I'd done something.

Eileen eventually remarried, around the time my parents
married. Her new husband was a farmer.

He was a good man,
but not really there.
He'd checked out a long time ago.

Eileen and I would sit on that porch and listen to the wind
while he sat in his chair in the house and watched television.

There she was,
way out on that farm,
with a man who spent most of his days in that chair.

And then I'd show up, bursting in with all my angst and
ache and curiosity and laughs.
Into that quiet farmhouse.
Into that lifeless marriage.
I see what was going on there,
what we were to each other.

She wasn't an effusive person, but I knew she believed in
me. I needed that. She didn't go on about it. It was a quiet
conviction. But I knew.

And then when I was twenty-one I was teaching water-
skiing at a camp in northern Wisconsin. On Sunday
mornings, they held a chapel service outdoors in a grove
of pine trees for everybody who worked at the camp. One
week the people who ran the camp asked if anyone wanted
to give the talk that coming Sunday. I volunteered. This
wasn't something I'd ever done before. Messages, sermons,

teachings, spiritual talks—there are a number of different words for it—that was all new to me.

You stand up in front of a group of people and you say something helpful or inspiring or profound about God and life and death and how to live?

How does a person do that?

Where do you even start?

And yet something within me was curious: *What would it be like to try that?*

And then Sunday came. I wore a maroon shirt with swordfish printed all over it and Birkenstock sandals. As soon as I walked up in front of those people sitting on those benches made of logs, I took off my sandals before I started talking because I had this sense that the ground had shifted beneath my feet and I was on sacred ground and my life was never going to be the same again.

It was that clear.

It was terrifying and thrilling, and it felt like coming home.

And I loved it. Immediately.

Like everything in my life up to that moment had been leading to *this*.

I had heard people give messages and teachings and sermons over the years. I usually didn't find them that compelling. But this, this SPIRITUAL TALK THING I had stumbled into—this was part guerrilla theater and part performance art and part recovery meeting and part poetry and part subversive rhetoric. I was captivated.

This is what I'm going to do with my life, I decided.

Several years after that, my grandma and I ended up living

near each other, and we started having lunch together every
Friday. We did that for the last ten years of her life.
She was there when I started my first job as a pastor,
listening to me give those first talks. I was driven to
explore this art form and take it places it hadn't been
before, and I threw myself into it, with her somewhere in
the audience.

She witnessed so many of those early bombs. All those
frenetic bursts and flying attempts at inspiring people. The
flamethrower. The giant pile of dirt. The time I brought out
all those live animals to make a point about something, and
they began defecating all over the stage. The time I dressed
up like a sheriff to illustrate something but I didn't explain
adequately enough why I was dressed up like a sheriff,
so much so that at the end of the sermon someone in the
audience asked,

Why are you dressed up like a sheriff?

I was so humiliated.
Standing up there sweating in that itchy, pale brown
uniform, feeling that hot shame of failure, wondering,
Who do I think I am to be doing this? Am I wasting my time?

Eileen saw it all.

I don't know how much she understood what I was trying
to do, but she showed up every time I was speaking. Even

when she stopped driving, her ninety-two-year-old friend
Helene—who still drove—would bring her.

She'd sit there and beam.

My dad, he has very few positive memories of his father,
Preston, before he died. He remembers a letter that Preston
sent to his parents, complaining to them about the behavior
of my dad and his brother. He remembers a man who acted
like his sons were a disruption in his life.

But Eileen, she idolized Preston.
She told me, *He was too good for this world.*
That's why he was taken away so young, was her explanation
for his early death.

And then I'm there,
right there in the midst of those two,
giving those talks.
And laughing.

Their losses shaped me. I never met Preston or Douglas, and
yet they've been present in my life from the beginning.
Their
absence
has been a form of
presence.

And that presence in absence tuned my ear to the pains
and paradoxes of life. Whatever the formula or explanation

or guarantee someone was giving, I always sensed things were more complicated than that, more tenuous, more mysterious—I wonder how much of that stems from the trauma Eileen and my dad had endured that still flowed in the family blood. My blood. I intuitively picked up on the inherent frailty and absurdity of this experience we're all having here, how quickly it can turn dark and tragic and crush your heart. I was surrounded by love and support, but what I knew from the story I had entered into was that all of it can be taken away in an instant.

However solid life may appear,
it's also very, very fragile.

And then my wife, Kristen, and I had our first child. We named him Robert Holmes Bell the Third. We call him Trace—*three* is *tres* in Spanish. There's this moment when we're there in the hospital and we introduce our new boy to my dad.

Robert Senior, meet Robert the Third.

I can feel the generations in that moment, like something is continuing, like I'm part of some great chain that extends way beyond me.

I would sit there for hours next to his crib, staring at him, filled with so much love for this little baby who doesn't really do much of anything. It's intoxicating, this love that goes one way. He doesn't have to do anything and

I'm absolutely transfixed. I have this sense all those hours watching him sleep that he's here to teach me something.

And then when our second son is born in April of 2000 there's this moment when I introduce my dad to his newest grandson.

Dad, this is *Preston Douglas Bell.*

I watch my dad's face as I say those two names together
Preston,
Douglas . . .
his father,
his brother,
all that past,
all that loss,
suddenly, swiftly brought into our midst,
right there in that hospital room.

I want it all there in that room,
I want it all coming back,
I want to see his face as I say those names.
It's like it's all looping back in on itself,
these multiple generations of souls,
all mingling and interacting.

Eileen was asked by her parents each night when she went to bed,
What did you do today to earn your keep?

I had heard that story growing up, but it was just that: a story. Until I began to struggle. I had this engine I couldn't turn off, this insatiable drive leading me to push myself way beyond what I could sustainably handle. Work, work, work. *Whatever you do just keep going, stay a step ahead of the ache.*

In my first job as a pastor one of my responsibilities was doing weddings. One Saturday I conducted three wedding ceremonies. For three different couples, in three different locations. I think about that now and I laugh. Apparently when the second couple asked about that particular date, instead of saying,
I'm sorry, I'm already doing a wedding that day
I said,
What time do you have in mind?

That story perfectly encapsulates how I didn't know how to step back, how to pause, how to turn the engine off. I just kept at it, pushing myself relentlessly. Taking on more and more and more. I would do a teaching on Wednesday night. And then another one on Saturday night. And then another one on Sunday morning. And then often another one on Sunday night. I did this for years. It was like I was trying to earn something that remained unearnable.

Eventually I crashed.
I burned out.
I was just so exhausted.

I ended up in the fetal position on the floor of my office, numb, wondering where it all went wrong.

I started looking for answers. And it's there, in that quest, that I began to see this larger story unfolding across multiple generations.

I recalled that story about Eileen being asked,
What have you done today to earn your keep?
I saw this generational lack of grace.
Love, yes.
But also this soul-crushing need to prove and earn and accomplish.

What do you do with the pain of life?
You keep moving, keep accomplishing, keep striving.
Whatever you do, don't be lazy. Don't appear to be coasting.
And whatever happens, stay a step ahead of the pain. Keep it buried. Keep it down.

My dad used to tell me,
You can find a lot of people who are smarter than me, but you'll never find someone who's worked harder.

As a kid, that sounded so impressive. My dad was already larger than life to me, and words like those made him loom even larger.

But when things began to fall apart for me and I went back into the heart of those messages I'd picked up over

the years, I started to see what else was lurking in there.
It was like this message had gotten imprinted on my cells:
*Whatever you do keep going, because if you slow down and
actually feel it all, who knows where that might lead?*

Through the help of a number of guides over a number
of years, I begin to see a new way to be, one rooted in the
enduring truth:
There's nothing to prove.

I see this chain of souls,
from one generation to the next,
I see what I've been handed,
I see what I can set down.
I see what I don't have to carry around anymore.

I continually notice how much I'm learning from my
boys. To love them as they find their way in the world is to
see myself, finding my way. I see
me
in
them
and how beautiful and refining all that angst and
exploration was. They help me embrace every last little bit of
my history. I see that it was all part of it. All that wondering
and wandering. They show me that it was all good, even
when it wasn't.

I come across an old newspaper clipping that I hadn't ever
seen. It's an article about Eileen and how she was traveling

around in the early '60s speaking to various groups about
nutrition and consumer goods. She was on the radio, she did
interviews.

She did?
As a single mom she built a career as a traveling speaker in
the '60s?
She never said anything about that.
What else have I missed?

Eileen and I were born fifty years apart.
From her mother to my daughter will cover the end of the
1800s to the beginning of the 2100s.
Preston died twenty years before I was born,
which was fifty years before our Preston was born.

I remember going to visit Eileen on August 22, 2008. We
knew she was close to the end, but I wasn't prepared for
what I experienced when we entered her room.
She was there on the bed,
but she wasn't there.
She was present, taking long, slow breaths,
but the part of her that made her, *her* was absent.
Like she'd already left.
I froze.
You know someone you love is going to die,
but then the day comes and nothing prepares you for *that*.

I stood there, not knowing what to do.
Kristen walked right over to her bed,

sat down next her,
held her hands, and then leaned in close over Eileen's heart,
saying in the most calming voice,
We're here, and we can see that you're leaving us, and we want
you to know how much we love you and how great these years
have been with you, and now we're letting you go . . .

It was as moving as it sounds.
Eileen died a few hours later,
on my birthday.

I give the eulogy at Eileen's funeral. Afterward we gather at
the Bell family burial plots in the town of Williamston. We
drop flowers on her casket after it's lowered into the earth.
We say a prayer. Eileen's sister, Maxine, sits in the front row,
repeatedly mumbling under her breath,

We had so many secrets, we had so many secrets . . .

They did?

The memorial is over, and everybody is making their way
back to the cars until it's just my dad and me, standing there
side by side over the open grave. He's quiet for a while, and
then he turns to me and says,
There are some things I want to tell you about what happened
when my dad died and when my brother died.

I knew it.
I knew there was more.

Shortly after that he gathers the family together and he pulls out a stack of photos. I haven't seen these pictures before. Pictures of him with his father, pictures of him with his brother. He describes in detail what it was like to stand there while the ambulance drove away. I'd heard bits and pieces over the years, but not from him, and never the whole story. He relives the few memories he has of his father. He shows us a picture of him and his brother in a boat on the river near their house.

He finishes and then he says,
Now, there are no more secrets.
He looks around at all of us.
He pauses.
And then he cries.
It's the first time I've ever seen my father cry.

In that moment he becomes a miracle to me.

I see how easily he could have taken another path. Despair. Hopelessness. The pain could have broken him.

But it didn't.
He channeled all that into a nuclear drive to work and achieve and serve the greater good and be the father to me and my sister, Ruth, and my brother, Jon, that he never had.

As I sit there witnessing his tears for the first time, I see how all that order and structure and success and striving and

law—my dad was a judge for forty-four years—and religion
and rules and everything else I chafed against from time
to time, I see how it helped him. I see what it was for him,
how it gave his life form and direction. I see the abyss he was
determined to climb out of. I see where the sheer intensity of
all that output came from. I gain a more expanded sense of
the scale of this story that I'm a part of as it's been unfolding
across the years.

My hearts breaks in that moment, in a good way. There's
something miraculous about all of it that comes crashing
down on me. Not just him, and the path he took, but my
own existence.

I'm here.
What a wondrous fact.
We're all here.
What an astonishing phenomenon.

And that farmhouse with the porch that Eileen and I used to
sit on when I visited her? That's the house my parents were
living in *when I was conceived.*

And then our daughter, Violet,
who's middle name is
Eileen
is with me at Starbucks just before I start writing this book,
and when they ask for the name on the order she says,
Eileen.

*   *   *

I tell you all this about where I come from and who I come from because you're like me.
We come from somewhere.
We come from somebody. Some *bodies*.
We're born into something.
It's already in motion.
Like a play and we stumbled onto the stage somewhere in the middle of the second act.
A child is like a blank slate?
No.
Our lives are loaded from the beginning with history and drama and love and wounds and tragedy and hope. I'm mysterious enough to myself, let alone the ones I come from, let alone all the people I'm constantly encountering with your own hopes and fears and histories and mysteries, let alone this floating ball of rock we call home that's hurtling through space at 67,000 miles per hour.

There is something infinite about all of it.
We never stop learning who we are and how we've been shaped by the people and places we come from.
Our hearts and minds and memories are endlessly explorable, there's more than enough to discover for one lifetime.
And that's just us.
If we move beyond ourselves,
to the world around us,
it's staggering . . .

All the galaxies in the universe are moving away from all
the other galaxies in the universe because the whole thing
has been expanding for thirteen billion years—
What?
Our galaxy, the Milky Way, the one we call home, is
traveling at around 500,000 miles per hour? Why? Where is
it going?
And apparently the sun is going to burn out in around five
billion years?
So this doesn't go on forever?
It has an . . . *end?*
And time, we now know, is actually a persistent illusion?
What we understand as past and present and future all exist
within some sort of *eternal now?*
What?
And we're each made of billions and billions and billions of
atoms, because everything, everywhere is made of atoms?
And atoms aren't really things or stuff at all but more like
relationships of energy or clouds of possibilities that are
mostly made up of empty space?

What an astonishing phenomenon this is,
this life that we find ourselves in.

Of course we have lots of questions.
Of course it's easy to feel lost and overwhelmed.
Of course when we see the first pictures ever of a black hole
the best we can come up with is *Wow.*
*What else does one say about something that no one has ever
seen before ever?*

Of course we wonder if there's any point to any of it.
Of course it means the world to us when we find out that
someone else feels what we feel.
Of course we experience terror and joy and hope and
despair, sometimes all in the same day.
Of course we sense that there's more going on here.

I've had this sense since I was young,
this conviction that there's more going on here,
that the world is not a cold, dead place,
but a dynamic reality that's way more interesting and
mysterious than anyone ever told us.

This book is about *that* sense.
I've tried to listen to it,
and trust it,
and follow it—
this awareness that everything is connected to everything else,
that it all matters,
that it's all headed somewhere.
It's taken me to places I never could have imagined,
places where the personal and cosmic connect,
where I've seen how that which is most intimate is also
universal, where that which is most particular to me is also
common to everybody.

I didn't know that my life could go this way—
that it could get
more compelling,
more meaningful,

more mysterious,
more surprising,
more fascinating year after year.

It's like an endless invitation,
this experience that we're having here,
and we can say yes,
over and over and over again.
And when we do, it opens up new depths, new connections,
and new possibilities we never could have imagined . . .

I grew up on a farm. Kind of.
When I was five, we moved into a turn-of-the-century
farmhouse on ten acres of land surrounded by suburban
neighborhoods. There was a barn and a granary and a chicken
coop and seven acres of alfalfa fields and three acres of lawn
and fifty cherry trees and fifty apple trees. At one point we
had seventeen cats that we would feed outside the back door.
We had a John Deere tractor. Sometimes I would go to soccer
practice and then come home and we'd bail hay. I went to
piano lessons *and* I knew how to operate the three-point hitch
on a combine. We didn't have cows or chickens or horses,
but I did have BMX ramps in the barn.

We had a rock boat.

A rock boat is a large metal sled that gets pulled behind a
tractor. One person would drive while the others would
walk behind the rock boat, picking up rocks from the field

and loading them on to the rock boat so that when it came time to plow that field there would be fewer rocks to slow the plow down. It was exhausting, and strangely hypnotic, following that rock boat around those fields, jamming your hands down into the soil, getting a good grip on the rocks, lifting them up out of the earth and onto that rock boat.

I remember the smell of that Michigan soil. The way the rocks would scrape the palms of my hands. The field mice that would race to get out of the way of the tractor tires. The sun setting as we made our way down the slope in the back field.

We played hockey on the pond across the road. The ice on that pond made a distinct sound when it cracked and my friend Ray fell through. He climbed out of the water and back onto the ice and kept playing with his pants frozen solid.

We had a dog named California Sunshine. I loved that dog. I loved that dog so much I had a yellow shirt that I wore every day with an iron-on appliqué on the front that said I LOVE MY DOG. I came home from school one day in the fourth grade and my parents were waiting for my sister Ruth and me. They told us that Sunshine had been hit by a car and died. We all walked out to the back field where my dad had dug a hole. Sunshine lay there lifeless. We cried for a while and then lowered her down into the earth. *That sound of the shovel lifting that dirt on top of her body.* It was the saddest I'd ever been.

When I was seven, my parents bought a six-hundred-square-foot cabin in the Upper Peninsula of Michigan five hours north of where we lived. That cabin, which didn't have a phone or television, was on a small lake in the middle of three thousand acres of national forest. We spent most of each summer at that cabin, going days without wearing shoes, swimming and hunting frogs and running around in the woods. It was too remote for a garbage truck—the nearest grocery store was forty-five minutes away—so the people around the lake dug a massive hole out in the woods. We'd throw our trash into it and then once in a while they'd set the hole on fire.

It was called the Dump.

Sometimes in the evenings after dark we would drive out to the Dump and sit there next to that big hole, quiet, waiting and hoping that a bear would come and pick through the trash.

Which happened regularly. We'd all be sitting there in our 1982 maroon Chevrolet Caprice Classic station wagon with a bear just a few feet away, doing our best not to make any noise. Paralyzed with an adrenalized mix of fear and fascination.

And then there was the water. I loved the water. I started water-skiing when I was eight, and when I was fourteen I learned to barefoot. Barefooting is when you water-ski without skis. The boat goes really fast and you skim across the water on your bare feet. It was a singular experience for me growing up, nothing could compete with that sensation. The boat would go into a tight turn, and I would let the momentum of the turn slingshot me way outside the wake. I'd been told that you could double the boat speed if you did it right. My feet sliding across the surface of the water somewhere over fifty miles an hour took me to someplace beyond words.

Sand, soil, water, trees, dogs, rocks, bears, woods, bales of hay, my feet skimming across the surface of the lake—I grew up with a visceral sense of connection to the earth. Those places and spaces I come from shaped me, like they were telling me in an endless number of ways that I was a part of it. Part of the land. Part of everything. Like we shared something. Like it was alive. Like it had something to say.

I had this feeling that there was something happening here, in this—this stuff, this matter, this thingness that you can hold and poke and carry and feel that is what bodies and land and air and sun and water are made of.

To this day water is where things make the most sense to me. I put my wet suit on and carry my board across the sand and into the ocean near where we live in Los Angeles.
As I paddle out I
always,
always,

always
feel like everything is beginning again. The smell of the
surf wax, the dolphin that just swam by, that sound of the
shoulder of a wave breaking just behind me as I glide across
the face. That orbital, swirling pattern of energy propelling
me across the surface of the earth. It not only never gets old,
it gets newer every time.

**When I was a kid my parents took us to church. I found
much of it rather uninspiring, but those Jesus stories, they
did something to me.**
What struck me in those stories was how the biggest
mysteries are found in the smallest things. A woman kneads
some dough, a party needs more wine. A man buries a seed,
rocks cry out. Something infinite happening in all that dirt
and sweat and stuff of life. Blood and crowds and roads
and friends—in those Jesus stories that's where the life, the
action, the divine is found.

I assume I wouldn't have articulated it like that as a kid, I
probably would have simply said that I sensed
there's more going on here.

That's why I resonated with those Jesus stories. Because in
them there's always more going on here.

Hints of something timeless and universal in a father waiting
for his son to come home. Signs of something infinite in the
ache of a woman who's sick and can't get well. They spoke

to my suspicion that there was a hidden depth to things. So much of the world I inhabited was a closed system, everything reduced to what could be measured and understood. What you could get your mind around. What could be grasped. What was practical. What produced results. What was efficient. What fit. How well I did on the test. How I measured up.

But those stories, it's like they cracked open a door to another room. There's a lot to find fault with in that particular expression of religious faith I grew up around, a lot that I don't find that compelling.

What is compelling to me is how those images and parables and phrases and hints struck a chord, subversively working their power and magic on me. My sense that there was an energy, a current, a pulse running through all of it was validated and affirmed. This place, here and now, this world, this is where the ultimate is found, this is where you find the truth. The mystery shows up in bodies. That connection I felt to the land and water and soil could be trusted, that's the message I absorbed. I realize now that an awareness was forming within me that the whole thing is alive in a subtle and profound and enduring way.

I had a best friend in junior high whose family had a cabin just a few doors down from ours.
We spent a good chunk of our summers together. I loved being with him, but something was off about his behavior. I didn't know what it was, but I knew it was something.

The people in a neighboring cabin arrived home one day to discover that the furniture on their deck had been smashed to pieces. This was big news around the lake. The rumor was that whoever did it used an ax. He and I talked about this for hours, endlessly speculating on who did it. He got a huge thrill from all that guessing and discussing.

And then one day his dad called my dad to tell him they'd checked him into a long-term-care facility for kids with mental illness. And yes, he was the one who had used an ax to destroy all that furniture.

It made sense, when I heard it.
All those strange moments,
all those inexplicable things he said and did.
It made sense, but it also didn't make sense.
This happened to my friend?
It left me with this chilling sobering feeling that anything could happen to anybody.

And then the parents of another friend of mine got divorced. That wasn't that unusual. But it was the details that killed me. His dad was moving out, loading his things into his car in the driveway, while he stood on the front lawn begging his dad not to leave. Bag after bag, box after box, my friend desperately pleading with his dad not to get in the car. And then his dad got in the car and drove away.

These experiences I had as a kid made me feel like the whole thing was unnervingly loose and unrestrained, like it was permeated with a freedom that meant anything could happen to anybody, like the world can do whatever it wants to whomever it wants whenever it wants.

Same with people.
We're free to do whatever we want.
Love, hate, build, tear down.
We can stay, or we can get in the car and drive away.

The world is free to be a world.
It's free to be beautiful and safe,
and it's free to break your heart in a thousand ways.
That free.

We ate dinner as a family most nights. We would talk nonstop through the entire meal. It was assumed around that table that everybody had something to say and everybody else was interested.

We'd ask my dad how his day was. As a judge, he spent most of his days in a courtroom hearing cases, talking to juries, meeting with lawyers. He always had stories to tell. When I was nine he had a murder trial in which a woman stabbed her boyfriend to death, chopping off his penis in the process. That one made an impression on me. Often his cases were in the news. Sometimes there would be extra security for him if there was a higher-than-normal number of death threats on his life. My mom attended a murder trial in his courtroom once and then told us later what it was like to hear the jury say *death penalty* and then hear everybody in the courtroom gasp.

Hearing those stories at dinner, and then often reading about them in the newspaper the next day, impressed upon me the reality of evil. My dad didn't make a big deal of it, but just telling us about whatever it was the person did who was in front of him on trial that day was enough. This freedom that we all have to do what we want, to act in many different ways, this freedom can lead to unspeakably horrific acts. I picked that up very clearly.

I never found the *why* questions of suffering and evil that interesting.
I still don't.
Why do bad things happen to good people? Why did she get cancer? Why did that earthquake kill all those people?
Those sorts of questions.
They've never held my attention for very long.

I assume this lack of interest is connected with my dad's loss of his father and brother. From an early age I knew that some people were missing.
From *his* youth,
from *our* life.
That presence in absence of Preston and Douglas was real. I could feel it. And there weren't ever going to be any answers or explanations. It was clear to me there's a randomness woven into the fabric of life, an uncertainty simmering just

below the surface, and often there is no *why*. Whatever it was, *it just happened.*

What was also clear to me was that my dad had set out to be the father he never had. And Ruth and Jon and I were the recipients of that love and determination.

Why wasn't that interesting to me,
but *what*—
What he did in response to that.
What happened after that.
What those losses led to—
the *what* questions were fascinating to me.
Something horrible happened.
Now what?
What's going to come out of this?
What's going to happen in response to it?
What new thing is going to be birthed out of this pain and loss?
Those questions captivated me.
They still do.

When I was in high school my parents had this friend whose husband decided he didn't want to be married to her anymore. She used to come over to our house and talk with my parents. I'd see her car pull up on the street, and then she'd get out and start walking up the driveway. You could tell from a hundred feet away how sad she was. She'd sit in a chair in our living room and my parents would sit on the couch and she'd talk and they'd listen. This would go on for hours. Then she'd get up and they'd embrace and she'd leave. And then she'd come back a few weeks later.

She became a symbol to me,
a sign of how quickly a person's life can turn.
You love somebody,
and then they decide they love someone else,
and then you're alone.

I was struck with how my parents would sit with her for so long, so often. It didn't seem like they were fixing anything, yet she kept coming back.

There was something going on there in that ritual of theirs.
Her pain, their love.
Her devastation, their availability.
Her talking, their listening.

There was something about the physicality of it, those bodies in that room, the way my parents were present with her. Something infinite there, showing up in all that sitting and listening. It spoke to me of the mystery that is born in bodies.

We'd visit a church service and I'd hear big, bulky words about God and heaven and judgment and salvation, and it all sounded a bit vague to me, like abstract concepts you could take or leave.

But being there for someone in pain,
that was concrete.
I could see it, feel it, grasp it.

It's personal.
That's what was formed in me.
A conviction that whoever or whatever God is or isn't or, to
say it another way, whatever is *ultimate* about life, it must
be personal. Personal, and *here,* in this place. Now. With us.
Something involving the earth. And touch. And couches.
And pain. And solidarity. And listening. And joining. And
presence.

Interesting, isn't it—how many of the seeds of the people we
become are planted early on in our lives?

And then I saw Midnight Oil.
My friend Dave got me a ticket. We were in our second year
of college in Chicago, and the Australian band Midnight
Oil were playing the Aragon Ballroom in support of their
latest album, *Diesel and Dust.* The lights went down, the
crowd roared, and we were blasted with a wall of sound.
The lead singer, Peter Garrett, is really tall and really bald,
and the second the band kicked in he started dancing and I
was stunned.

I'd never seen anything like it.
Peter Garrett stalked the stage like he owned it.
It was so intense.

He jerked, he floated, he twitched, he gestured.
That band was ferocious.
I was transfixed.

They sang songs about indigenous rights and corporate
greed and the exploitation of the earth and the failure of
governments to protect the vulnerable.

It was righteous and angry and passionate. I'd seen some
of that before—I'd seen people fighting for a cause, I'd seen
people standing up against injustice.

But this, this was different.
Midnight Oil did it with *joy.*
I hadn't seen those two together like this before.
Resistance *and* joy.
Defiance *and* euphoria.
Subversion *and* celebration.

They were naming all this violence and injustice that we've
done to each other and the earth, but instead of being an
abrasive turnoff, like we were being harangued or preached
at, it was intoxicating.

I'd heard guilt trips before. I'd heard speakers and
coaches and teachers and religious leaders work
themselves into a frenzy trying to get people to do more,
try more, care more, work more—I once had a soccer
coach who would take off on one of the players' mopeds
and we had to chase him.

For miles.
And if anyone wasn't keeping up,
he'd go *faster*.

Kids would be throwing up,
bent over heaving,
and he'd be yelling at us about how we didn't want it bad
enough.

I'd seen people do all kinds of manipulative things to try to
motivate and inspire.

But this, this thing Midnight Oil was doing,
these songs they were singing,
this potent cocktail of joy and subversive resistance,
this passion yoked to a cause,
all that noise giving voice to the voiceless,
this moved me,
it pulled me in,
it made me want to do more, know more, be more.
It stirred in me this desire to give my life to something
bigger than my life.
There was something inviting about it, like their passion and
focus had this subtly implicit undercurrent to it, insisting
that I could find my thing and give myself to it, whatever it
was, like they were . . .

Around that time Dave and our friends Toby and Steve
started a band. They found a drummer they called
Hawg. They had written all this great music, but they

didn't have a singer or any lyrics. So they held auditions
to find a front man for their band. One fella showed up
for his audition, stood there at the mic brushing his long
blond hair back from his face, but when it came time to
sing, he was unable to come up with any words for their
songs.

He has nothing to say?
He has this incredible opportunity,
he literally *has the mic,*
but he can't find anything to sing?
I was dumbfounded.

I was also obnoxious, slouching there in the corner,
watching those auditions. Of course I had zero experience
doing anything like that, but it didn't keep me from offering
a withering critique.

At one point someone suggested that I try to be the singer. I
don't know whose idea it was, probably mine.
But I suspect my friends wanted me to try it just to end their
misery.

I scratched out pages of lyrics,
stepped up to the mic,
and out came a torrent of high-pitched sing/song/rap/
rhyme/rant/storytelling/gibberish that strangely . . . *worked.*
We all looked around at each other when the first song was
done and smiled, tentatively, as if asking,
What was that?

Because it was *something.*

In that moment, Ton Bundle was born. We went on to write songs and play shows and record EPs and an album. I wrote lyrics that the crowd would sing back to us. I became convinced we were going to be the next great band. I talked about it all the time, how we were going to *make it.* That was the phrase I repeated over and over to anyone who would listen. *Make it.* It's all I wanted to do.

That feeling of creating something, of taking what was happening inside me and around me and giving it words and then sharing it with people, I'd never experienced anything like it. It made me feel like I might actually have something to contribute to the world.

And those gigs, they were like a tribal fire, all those kids crammed in those tight spaces, bodies pressed up against bodies. My job was to bring everybody in, to help everybody feel a part of it. To reach all the way to the back of the room and connect. To move all that energy around the room. To help us feel as one.

There was something terrifyingly vulnerable about it, something I loved,
something I found intoxicating.
We'd walk out on the stage and I'd step up to the mic and I'd look out at all those eyes looking back at us and the first song would start—

those gigs demanded unflinching commitment.
Like jumping off a cliff.
You leap, and you can't look back.
If you don't give it everything you have, everybody knows.
We're hypertured in to energies—we know when someone
is holding back. When they're scared. When they're not
giving it their all.

There were these shows called Cool Aids—six or seven punk
bands playing back-to-back in a basement, all the money
going to charity. (Because it's COOL to give AID.) One show
we came out and the band started playing and I jumped up
and kicked the ceiling—I could do the splits at that time,
a standard tool in the lead singer toolbox—and the ceiling
tiles shattered and sent plaster and dust all over the front of
the crowd.
It was glorious.
And it was shaping how I saw the world.
Because any idea we came up with we could try.
Someone would throw out a suggestion and we'd all laugh
at how absurd it was and then we'd laugh a little less as we
thought,
Well, why not? We should at least try it . . .

This was revolutionary for me.

So much of life felt like it was decided by others. You go to
class and the professor tells you what the assignments are
and when the exams are. You get a job and someone tells
you what to do. Everywhere I'd turn there was an authority

figure pointing to a map or a list of rules or a manual, reminding me that this is how things are to be done.

But in that band we could come up with something and then do it, whatever it was. We had this friend named Charlie who was doing these huge oil paintings of monsters with giant tongues and bulging eyeballs. Our friend Claris was a genuine opera singer. Our friend Greg started wearing overalls with no shirt underneath and fronting a country music cover band. My roommate Ian was recording techno albums in our apartment. Our friends Theo and Kristofer and Dan had a band called The Gadflys—their songs are still in my head to this day. These were the people I was surrounded by, endlessly making things and sharing them with the world around us.

Our senior year of college we lined the walls of the basement of the house we lived in with carpeting foam we'd found by the side of the road and then we spray-painted all that foam a deep shade of red. It was our rehearsal space. We called it the Tummy.

In the Tummy, anything was possible. We were free to conjure up new worlds, as absurd and bizarre and heartfelt and earnest as we could imagine. And we didn't need permission. We didn't have to get approval. We got an idea and then we did the work to bring it to life.

They were just four-minute songs, but they were teaching me how creation works. We didn't have to wait to see what happened, we could create the happening.

We'd make something, and then we'd share it, and we'd
all feel this connection, like there we were all caught up in
something bigger than ourselves.

All that creation
and all that connection.
What a gift.
To be in that band.

We got a manager the fall of our senior year. He got us
several gigs at the best clubs in Chicago. We were on our
way.

And then one Friday night I got a headache. I took some
aspirin. The headache got worse. My friends went out
but I stayed home, lying there on the couch with that
headache. By the middle of the night I hadn't slept, the
pain getting worse by the hour. I sat on the floor of
the downstairs bathroom, wondering if I was dying.
As the sun came up I asked my roommate Ian to take
me to the hospital. They did test after test, and then
a neurologist came in and told me that I had viral
meningitis. He explained that the fluid around my brain
was infected and swollen and it was squeezing my brain
against the walls of my skull.

So that's what that was.
To this day, every person I've ever met who has had viral
meningitis says the same thing:
You feel like you're going to die.

I had to stay in the hospital for a while, which meant Ton Bundle had to cancel those gigs.

I was devastated.

Not just about those gigs but about this growing awareness I had that it was over. It wasn't just that those gigs were canceled, it was this ominous sense I had that the band was going to end. I knew it. Graduation was looming, and that meant jobs and futures and new responsibilities. College bands rarely survive those pressures.

I lay there in that hospital bed completely lost. I kept repeating these two words to no one in particular:
Now what?

I realize now that those two words were forming a prayer.
Now what?
In a visceral way, prayer is naming what matters to you.
Now what? is what mattered to me.
I had all this energy and passion and desire to give myself to something, and now I had nothing.
It was a gut-wrenching question, that
Now what?
A full-bodied, desperate plea.
It was angry and impotent and honest.

I had no plan B.
I didn't get good grades in college, I didn't really have a résumé. I'd started a painting company called Skinny Boy Painting that I ran in the summers. And by company, I

mean *me*. I was my only employee. I didn't see myself doing that next.

Now what? was all I could muster up.

It's at the end of ourselves that new futures open up.
Our plans fall apart. Our strength isn't enough. Our cleverness fails us.
Now what?
That's universal.
You cry out like that and you're joining a long line of souls from across the ages.
I'd heard people ask questions about prayer.
Does God hear our prayers?
Does prayer work?
What if you pray and you don't get an answer?

I never found those questions that interesting. It felt like they turned the great mystery into a vending machine. Say or do or believe or ask for the right thing and then you'll get what you want. Or you won't. That sort of thing.

But that *Now what?* prayer,
that prayer changed me.

There was a world of confusion and longing and frustration trapped in my chest and that *Now what?* prayer dragged it all out in the open. It gave language to that black hole of despair. I was angry that the one thing that had ever really made me feel like I had something unique to contribute was being taken away from me and there was nothing I could do about it.

That prayer gave all that rage and grief and loss words. Day after day in that hospital bed, wondering what I was going to do with my life. Repeating those two words.

I eventually recovered and went back to school, but that prayer stayed with me. It gradually morphed from an anguished, bitter cry to a question, a quest, a line of inquiry.

As the emotion ebbed from it,
curiosity emerged.
Now what?
It's like those two words grew into the question they'd always been.

I started paying attention to my life in new ways.
I started looking for clues and direction.
I started listening more.

One day a girl I'd talked to maybe twice said to me,
Have you ever thought about being a pastor?
I laughed.
Not really.
A pastor.
I'd seen some pastors.

That wasn't really me.

Then something similar happened again, with someone else asking me if I'd thought about doing that.

It started to get weird.

This idea of being a pastor wouldn't go away.

I'd had this sense that there's more going on here for as long as I could remember. And there was a job where you helped people connect with that something more?

I had this image in my head of what a pastor was.

And I knew I couldn't do that.

But I could be me and try doing that.

That sounded like something I could give myself to.

Curiosity is underrated.

In many ways, it's the engine of life. You get these questions, and they don't go away. And so you follow them, you set out to answer them. And you get answers. And those answers, of course, lead to new questions. And on and on it goes.

There's a humility baked into curiosity.

You don't know—that's your starting point.

You're coming from a place of openness, driven by a conviction that there's something more, something beyond you, something else out there.

Curiosity is an antidote to despair.

Despair is the spiritual disease of believing that tomorrow will simply be a repeat of today. Nothing new. The future simply an unbroken string of todays, one after another. But curiosity, curiosity disrupts despair, insisting that tomorrow will not be a repeat of today. Curiosity whispers to you, *You're just getting started . . .*

I didn't want to live my life wondering,
What if . . . ?
I had seen people do that.
They had something nudging them in a particular direction, but they didn't follow it. They didn't take the risk. They didn't listen to their heart. And years later they felt stuck, wondering where it all went wrong.
I didn't want to live like that.
I wanted to know,
What if I tried that . . . ?

My mom's name is Helen, and she grew up in Southern California.
Her father, Neil, was born and raised in Denmark and came to America when he was nineteen, eventually settling in Los Angeles. He never went back to Denmark, even to visit, and never saw his parents again after he left. He eventually married my grandmother Ruth, an artist who lived by the ocean in Los Angeles. He called her Weefie. Her brother had died when he was four, her mother died when she was fifteen, and when she met Neil she was living with her father, taking care of him. Weefie had the best smile. Well into her eighties she could light up a room with that smile.

Every other year at Christmas we went to California to visit Neil and Ruth and the rest of my mom's side of the family. I loved those trips. The way the sun shone through the palm trees in the late afternoon, the curves in the 110 freeway, the ocean, the snow on Mount Wilson. I couldn't get enough of Los Angeles. I was entranced. I was from another place, but Los Angeles felt like the place I was from.

We'd go to the Van Doren Shoe Store on Colorado Boulevard so that Ruth and I could get a new pair of Vans. That store was shoe mecca for me. And the smell, *that smell*, the particular rubber smell of those soles. The whole store smelled like that. Pulling the shoes out of the box and smelling that smell. Keeping the box so I could open it back in Michigan and smell it all over again and be transported back to that store.

No one where I lived wore Vans. I would wear those shoes every day for years, hoping they'd last until it was time to go back to California.

We'd return to Michigan and I'd go to the Meridian Mall, where I'd read the newest issues of *Surfer* magazine, which they kept on the back shelf of the Community Newscenter bookstore. I'd leaf through those pages like they were a portal to another world, like I was seeing behind a veil. All those pictures of water and waves. I'd spend hours in the back of that bookstore, sitting on the floor, those magazines spread out on the floor around me.
I couldn't get California out of my head.

* * *

Some things speak to us, and they never stop speaking.
Longings, places, desires, questions about what our lives
could be and where they might go and who we could
become—they arise within us and they dwell there,
sometimes calmly, patiently, other times insistently tugging
on our sleeve, demanding that we give them a proper
hearing.
That's what happened to me.
This idea of being a pastor wouldn't go away,
and that meant I needed more school.
I applied to one seminary,
and I got in.
That seminary was in, of course, California.

But first, I headed to Wisconsin to teach water-skiing for
the summer . . .

**One day I'm sitting in a lecture hall in seminary, listening
to this esteemed British scholar go on about something
very important when he pauses and says *Roman Numeral
Four* and then he keeps talking.**
Wait—what? Roman Numeral *Four*? There were three
other Roman Numerals before this? He's working through
an outline? I scrambled through my notes, looking for the
structure, trying to figure out how this next section was
related to the previous section.

This particular professor was legendary. He'd written his own systematic theology, which in that world was a huge deal. Picture a row of large hardcover books, taking up about two feet on a shelf, all of that writing about *God*. Page after page, arranged and organized into topic and point and sub-point. Thousands of pages explaining the biggest ideas you can imagine. All written by him.

That's serious, and very impressive, and clearly we'd just ended the Roman Numeral Three part, and we were moving on to the Roman Numeral Four part, but I wasn't that moved. All those ideas, all those clarifications, all that structure and order—he was obviously brilliant, and I was learning so much, but there was something slightly lifeless about it.

A bit like a butterfly. You can capture a butterfly, and pin its wings down to study the colors and shape and design, but the moment that butterfly is still and you're able to make the most precise and detailed observations about that butterfly is the moment the butterfly can't fly anymore.

I was working with high school students at the time, helping out in a youth group at a church. There was a student whose parents were getting divorced, and he asked if he could come live with me for a while. His name was Matthew. He drove a vintage Willy's Jeep and wore a straw cowboy hat. I'd make him breakfast in the morning and make sure he had what he needed for the day at school. We'd eat dinner that evening and talk about what we'd done and who we'd seen that day. The two of us there in that apartment—I was twenty-two, he was sixteen. There was something tender about it, like it was the two of us against the world.

Around that time there was a big event going on at that church, and I was responsible for organizing the Saturday morning gathering for the students. When the students arrived, I gathered them around and told them that we were going to take a walk in the neighborhood. That was unusual for those kids, because that particular church was surrounded by neighborhoods very different from the neighborhoods they lived in. It was just a few blocks, but it was another world. I told them we were going to knock on doors and ask people if they needed anything.

That simple. And those students, they were up for it.

We started out. They knocked on the first door. A woman came to the door holding a baby on her hip. They asked her if she needed anything. She said yes, she needed milk for her baby. She explained to them that she'd been mixing sugar with water to feed the baby because she didn't have money for anything else.

The students were shocked. They immediately started discussing how much money they had and where the nearest

store was. They divided themselves up, some going to the
store, others staying with the mom, others going on to
the next house.

I stood in the street, smiling, knowing we'd be talking about
this day for a while.

There were eye-opening and euphoric experiences like that
one, there were also nightmares we went through together.
One of the students lost his mom. She was in the driveway
early one morning getting the newspaper when two men
ran by who'd just robbed the neighbor's house. When they
realized she'd gotten a good look at them, they shot and
killed her. Her husband found her there in the driveway,
and then he had to wake up each of his kids to tell them that
their mom had died. That student and I, we spent hours in
the following days driving around Los Angeles, processing
what had happened. He was talking, I was sitting there in
the front passenger seat, listening. Sometimes we'd just
listen to music while we drove along because there wasn't
anything left to say.

Moving back and forth between those two different
environments was doing something to me. In the one, I
was doing this academic work to earn a master's degree
in divinity, listening to lectures and writing papers
and learning Greek and Hebrew and studying maps
of the ancient world. And in the other I was spending
countless hours with those students, riding in cars and
hanging out in backyards and visiting their schools

and taking long walks through previously unexplored neighborhoods.

That academic work had a static dimension to it, like we were studying from a distance, analyzing and scrutinizing, making distinctions about distinctions. In that world I got points for precision, for my ability to parse and exegete and summarize. I was rewarded for how well I could pin the butterfly.

But with those students, it was all movement and motion. They had joys and pains and questions, and they wanted me to enter into all of it with them. Life with them felt like an endless invitation to participate. Like something was happening bigger than all of us, and why wouldn't you want to be a part of it?

My understanding of God was subtly shifting during that time. I had grown up with a more static view of a divine being who exists somewhere else and then intervenes in this world from time to time. That understanding was fading, being replaced with something more dynamic and vibrant and alive. Something less out there and more right here, right now. Something much less about pinning it down and much more about flying.

And then Kristen Childress showed up in Los Angeles. I'd known her for four years. We met our first week of college. She was from Arizona and told me she grew up water-skiing. I was impressed. We became friends.

I was always slightly intimidated by her. She carried herself with an elegance and dignity that made me feel like I was way out of my depth. She had this grounded, calming presence about her, like she knew who she was and she wasn't easily swayed by what everyone else was doing.

For four years, we were just friends. And then she called to tell me she was moving to Los Angeles to go to graduate school. She moved near me not long after that, and we fell in love—
there's so much there,
I don't know where to begin.
How do you put words to falling in love?
It was like coming home.
It was like finding my other half.
Even those images fall short.

There's this feeling you get when you hear certain classic songs, this sense that those songs have always existed and the songwriter somehow discovered them. That's what it was like. Like this thing—this energy, this exchange, this back-and-forth—this happening between us had always existed and we were just beginning to realize it.
Like it had always been.
Like it was brand-new,
and as old as the world,
at the same time.

One Saturday night we were discussing what we were going to do—make dinner and stay in? Drive out to see the sunset in Malibu? Take a stroll down Melrose? I remember us

talking about all those options and realizing in the midst of
that discussion that it didn't really matter. I was with her,
and everything would be fine, whatever we did.
This realization was massive for me.
It was just plans for an ordinary Saturday night, and yet that
discussion perfectly encapsulated our life together.
We'd be fine, whatever came our way.
Whatever we would go through.
We'd be all right, together.

We had this belief that the whole thing is an adventure,
and we had found someone to go on the adventure
with . . .

There was something lurking in her love for me,
something that took me a while to sort out.
She loved me exactly as I was.
She had no lists, no demands—there was nothing she said I
needed to do to improve.
It was unnerving at first.

I was so used to the inevitable *ands* . . .
You're loved, *and here's what you need to work on* . . .
You're loved, *and you should try harder* . . .
You're loved, *and if you'd just do more* . . .
That's how the world worked.
But not with her.
With her,
those *ands* never came.

There was a giant paradox there, hiding in that love.
She didn't make any demands, but what that did was make
me want to be a better person.
She loved me exactly as I was, but what that produced in me
was a tremendous desire to live up to that love.

Grace. That's a word for it.
She embodied this acceptance of me precisely as I was that
was surprisingly, inexplicably motivating.

Gospel. That's another word for it.
Gospel is the divine announcement that you are loved
and accepted exactly as you are, that everything has been
taken care of, that everything you've been striving to earn
has been yours the entire time, that you belong, in exactly
this condition that you are currently in, nothing additional
required or needed.

There was something *gospel-like* in this new love,
something that was grounding me in new ways.
This love,
her love,
my heart could hardly bear it.
It was like it was too good to be true.
It was such a mystery to me, how she had let go of any need
to have me be something or somebody other than I was, and
how that was paradoxically the very catalyst that made me
want to give myself to her and the world with everything I
had.

How did surrendering something cause that very thing to be
way more likely to happen?
How did not requiring me to do anything more produce in
me a nuclear desire to do more?

She was like an announcement,
or a question,
or a paradox,
or a divine disruption,
or a phenomenon.

Married is such an inadequate word for it.
More like *being caught up in something.*

I was studying all of these big ideas about gospel and Jesus
and grace in my coursework, but that was like peering
into a microscope or standing over a subject in a lab coat
compared to what I was experiencing with her.
It was the paradox of it that stayed with me, as if I were
hearing a whisper, quietly and calmly letting me know that
the whole thing worked in a very different way from what
anybody had ever told me.

During that first year we were together there were massive
forest fires in the San Gabriel Mountains just above where
we lived. We could see the flames and smell the smoke. One
evening I was at that church, getting ready for the youth
group that night, when the youth pastor pulled me aside. He
was giving the talk that night, and he wanted me to open
the shades on the windows of the top-story room we were

meeting in at a certain point in his talk. I didn't think much of it, assuming he had some point he wanted to make.

Which he did.

At the moment he had prepared me for he dramatically gestured toward the window, I opened the shades, and the students got a spectacular view of the mountain above us on fire. He then launched into a rant about hell and eternal suffering and torment and how if you didn't become a Christian and believe the right things and say the right prayer, then those flames on the mountain would be nothing compared to what you'd be experiencing forever when you died.

I was mortified.

I stood there in the back, shaking with rage watching those kids take it all in.

I was so angry.

I was just a twenty-three-year-old assistant in a youth group with little experience and no achievements to speak of. No one knew or cared what I had to say beyond maybe a handful of high school students once in a while. But a conviction was forming in me, a conviction that would only grow stronger as the years went on. If I ever got the microphone someday, if I ever got the chance to speak, it would be gospel. No fear, no guilt, no shame, no manipulation, no lists of what you have to do to earn what you already have—I resolved to do my best to announce that the good news is better than that,

that we've been loved the whole time and all that's left to do is trust that this is actually true and then live like it.

I was experiencing this truth in my new life with Kristen, and it was flowing over into my academic work and my life with those students. It was all becoming gospel—this joyous, counterintuitive, disruptive, surprising, searing announcement of divine love for everybody, everywhere. You could scare the hell out of someone for a minute or two, you could shame someone into changing their ways for a short time, you could use fear to accomplish a great number of things in the short run, but I was going to play a different game. I'd heard those Jesus stories since I was young, and they moved me and resonated with me, but now they were taking on a new weight in my life, like they weren't just stories, they were a way of life, a way of seeing the world, showing me something present in the elemental nature of the universe. If I ever got the chance, *that's* what I would talk about.

Ed Dobson was raised in Belfast, Northern Ireland, he was short, he had massive hands, and he spoke in a slow, deep voice.
My parents told me about him. They had moved to Grand Rapids, Michigan, while I was away at school, and they raved about his speaking. So the next time I visited them, I went to see for myself.

He was giving a sermon the first time I saw him, standing in his church on the front of the stage with the toes of his shoes sticking out over the edge, like he was about to fall off but he didn't. There was something slightly hypnotic and utterly compelling about how he communicated. He'd make a point, then he'd tell a story, then he'd ask a question, then he'd gesture with those massive hands.

I'd never seen anything like it.
I looked around. People were captivated, leaning forward in their seats, hanging on his every word.

I had to meet him.

There were thousands of people there—that was new to me, a crowd that big and that energized at a church service— and I assumed he was busy after he gave the sermon. I went looking for him anyway and found him in a room behind the stage. I introduced myself and then gave him a Ton Bundle album. On cassette.

He contacted me later to say he loved the album.
I wasn't expecting that.
And then we became friends.
And then he became a mentor.
And then he offered me my first job as a pastor.
What an opportunity.

We moved from California to Grand Rapids, Michigan. For Kristen, this was like moving to another planet. It took years for us to better understand her sense of alienation. In my excitement I didn't give that sense the weight it deserved. I loved my new job, and it drowned out a number of truths about our lives at that time.

It was all new, and I took every opportunity I could get. Funerals, weddings, hospital visits, prison visits. People in crisis. People who needed someone to walk with them through their traumas and tragedies. People asking big questions about life and death and everything in between.

And of course talks. Lots of talks and teachings. I would go anywhere and talk to any group of people. Fairs, basements, chapels, camps, schools, sports teams—anywhere they'd have me I'd show up with something to say.

It was the mid-'90s, in the Midwest, and that church was the biggest thing going for miles around. Thousands of people, services throughout the week, traffic jams getting in and out of the parking lot. That church was a *scene*.

And I got to be right in the middle of it,
following Ed around,
sitting in meetings with him,
asking questions,
learning so much.

I loved it.
I never knew what was going to happen on any given day.
What a thrill.

I slowly began to notice a pattern. I'd first seen it in the job
interview, months before I started. They asked me to talk
about my *call to ministry*. I'd heard that phrase before, it was
a way pastors described why they became pastors. They'd
tell a story, a sort of supernatural narrative about how God
had told them this is what they were supposed to do with
their life. The people interviewing me wanted to hear my
story about how I knew this is what I was supposed to do.

I didn't have one.
At least not like that.
That all seemed a bit presumptuous.
What about the people who had been *called* and they weren't
that good at being a pastor?
I'd seen that, and didn't want any part of it.
And claiming God had told you to do something?
I thought that was crazy.

And what about schoolteachers and nurses and people who
fix cars and build things? What about their calling?

Some people are called, and some aren't?
Some people do a special, elevated kind of work, and
everybody else does—what?—regular work?

I had stumbled into work I loved, and I was pursuing it
with everything I had. I had a driving curiosity to explore
this particular art form, and I had given myself to it. Love,
curiosity, passion, meaning, serving something bigger than

myself, hope—I didn't need more of a story than that. That was enough *calling* for me.

It was just one question in that job interview, and I was so happy to get a job anywhere that I didn't think much of it. But I noticed that the beliefs behind that question kept appearing in things people would say to me. Someone would tell me a story—a heartbreaking, inspiring, deeply moving story about something that mattered to them or something they'd survived or how much they loved someone in their life.
I'd be sitting there on the edge of my seat,
so moved,
and then they'd say something like,
But what do I know? I'm not a pastor, I'm just an insurance agent. Or a mom. Or a teacher. Or an accountant. Or a construction worker.

This happened often. Me, with my jaw on the floor, filled with wonder and awe from what I'd just heard. And the person sitting across from me, telling me that they didn't really know what they were talking about, they weren't an expert on any of this, it's not like they were a pastor or anything . . .

It felt like there was a glitch in the system, like there was this division lurking just below the surface, this separation between the ones who had been called and everybody else. It started with that question, but I began to see this division all over the place.

I was reading the Bible constantly because of all the talks
I was giving, and I kept stumbling across things I'd never
seen before. I had studied the Bible in seminary, but that
was in class. For a grade. This, this was different. This was
in the wild. This was reading to come up with things to say
and teach to real people in a real place. In many ways, I was
reading the Bible for the first time.

I saw that there's no word for *spiritual* in the Hebrew
scriptures (also called the Old Testament). So basic, and yet
so revolutionary. There's no word for *spiritual,* because to call
something spiritual would be to imply that other things *aren't.*

In the Bible, everything is spiritual.
All of life.

It's never *just a job,*
you're never *just* a mom or *just* a dad,
it's never *just* money,
it's never *just* your body.

Nothing exists in isolation,
it's all connected.

This blew my mind. And confirmed this growing sense I had
that things were way less separated than I had ever realized.

Business, politics, education, art, science, caring for the
earth, looking out for the poor, what you eat, where you go,
sex, music—it's all spiritual.

I saw how in the story about Moses and the burning bush,
Moses doesn't take his sandals off because suddenly the
ground becomes holy. The ground had been holy the
whole time. The story is about Moses becoming aware
of it.

I read the story in the book of Genesis about Jacob waking
up from a dream and saying, *Surely God was in this place,
and I, I wasn't aware of it.* Jacob is waking up from a dream,
but he's waking up in a larger sense as well, to the divine
presence in all of life.

I read in the Psalms, *The earth is the LORD's and everything
in it.*

The insistence, again and again, is that reality is not split, it's
one. All of life permeated with the divine presence, all of it
sacred.

I saw how the Bible isn't a book about how to get into
heaven, it's a library of poems and letters and stories about
bringing heaven to earth now, about this world becoming
more and more the place it should be. There is very, very
little in the Bible about what happens when you die. That's
not what the writers were focused on. Their interest, again
and again, is on how this world is arranged.
Does everyone have enough?
Are the power structures tilted in favor of the vulnerable?
*Has violence been renounced, or is it being kept in
circulation?*

I read the passage where Abraham argues with God. And
then I read where Moses argues with God. And then I read
those prayers in the Psalms with those lines
Where are you?
and
Why do you hide your face from me?
and
Why have you forsaken me?

People questioning God, doubting God, arguing with God.

This was honest,
and angry,
and challenging.
There was a back-and-forth here,
the divine and human,
in an endless conversation.
Like a dialogue.
Or a wrestling match.
Or a dance.

I saw how Jesus answered almost every question he's asked
with a question . . .
What do you think?
How do you read it?
How do you interpret it?
What do you say about it?

This is the opposite of brainwashing.
This is the opposite of

Just believe and don't ask questions.
He keeps inviting people to think critically, to examine, question, doubt, test, struggle.
To own it for themselves.
I came across this line in the New Testament:
Test everything.
I love that line.
It's so simple, and yet there's so much energy in it. The word
test
there in the original Greek could also be translated
to welcome.
It's this idea of welcoming the good wherever you find it, embracing it and celebrating it. It spoke to me of a certain intellectual rigor at the heart of life—you never just accept something because someone told you or someone said it's true. You test it, you poke, you prod, you see what it does in the world. How it shapes you. What it leads to.

Everything just kept getting more and more interesting.

I saw how the entire foundation of the book of Leviticus is grace. These slaves have been freed and they're given rituals to celebrate this newfound freedom and then organize their lives around it.

I saw how the word for *command* in Hebrew is the word *mitzvot,* and it can better be translated as *charge.* Like when you charge someone with an important task. Less something you're supposed to do and if you don't do

it you're going to be punished, and more like a sacred
responsibility that speaks to your deepest, truest self.

I saw how the name of God keeps changing—one person
uses this word, this group uses that word, later on they
name it something else. Elohim, Yahweh, Adonai, Theos—
the list goes on. I saw how each of these names comes
out of the particular struggles and hopes of that time
and place, reflecting economics and politics and shifting
consciousness. I saw how we've been trying to make sense
of the depths of life and what kind of universe it is that we're
living in for thousands of years.
This search and response and discovery and discussion and
exploration was way more alive,
way more fluid,
way more evolving than I had ever realized.
It was way more like life actually is—sweaty and disturbing
and maddening and elusive and wondrous and intoxicating.

The church I was working in did a survey to find out more
about the people who were coming to all those services. One
of the questions asked people how important their *spiritual
lives* were to them.
What? I thought.
Spiritual lives?
What other kind of life is there?

What this particular religious system that I was working
in did was ever so subtly divide the world up into two
spheres . . . the spiritual, and then the rest of life.

As if spiritual is a dimension of life that some people have, and some don't.

As if spiritual means less real than the stuff of everyday life like money and bodies and kids and houses and jobs.

As if spiritual is about another time and another place when you die and leave this place.

As if some people are spiritual, and some people aren't.

This split was subtle,
but it affected everything.
And what I kept reading in the Bible was story after story of people growing in their awareness of the connected, sacred, spiritual nature of all of life.

The church wanted to affirm me in a formal way, so they organized an ordination ceremony on a Sunday night. Before the ceremony, I was told there would be a daylong session where I'd be questioned about my beliefs and theological knowledge.

I was so curious.
I wonder what this will be like.

I showed up on that morning, and they started asking me questions. Technical questions about theology, hypothetical questions about books in the Bible. One question was about the distinction between ontological worth and ministerial function. Those sorts of questions.

This went on for hours.

Partway through it dawned on me: *None of these questions are about my life.* There wasn't one question along the lines of

Have you ever forgiven someone who's wronged you?

or

What are your fears?

or

Are you generous?

Not one question about how I actually lived my life. But there was one question:

What if an archaeologist unearthed a third letter to the Corinthians? What should we do with that?

However interesting that question might be to somebody, somewhere, it felt to me in that moment so far removed from the people I was interacting with every day.

I was ordained—a public confirmation of my role as a religious leader—without any discussion about whether or not I embodied the things that I was teaching and talking about.

I had given enough of the right answers,
and I knew enough of the right things,
and that was enough.

These were good people,
and I loved them and had great respect for them.
But the system we were all a part of,
the system had a glitch.

It split the world up.
This space, and then other spaces.
The sacred, and then the secular.
What you believe, and then how you actually live.
The called, and the not called.
Spiritual life, and then the rest of life.

Ed, it turns out, had a second office.
There was his regular office. It had a row of windows and a desk and a couch and chairs. There was a door in that office, and that door led to another office. That office didn't have any windows. It had a table and a chair and bookshelves.

That office was where Ed studied for his sermons.

It was like an inner sanctum,
or a secret chamber,
or a holy place,
where the leader goes in,
and gets the divine message,
and then brings it out and gives it to the people.

And only Ed went in there.

Until one day, in my third year with him, when he invited me into that office to study with him.

I'd been giving more and more teachings, often stepping in when he wasn't there, and he decided that we would study together and come up with a talk, and then he'd give it in some services and I'd give it in the others.

It was like being called up to the premier league. I tried to stay calm, but I was so excited.

We worked for hours on that sermon. We started with a verse in the Bible, and then we studied the context and the specific words, then we found themes and connections to other ideas and texts. We passed books back and forth, discussing what it meant. We identified the major points we wanted to make. An outline gradually emerged. What we'd say first, then what we'd say next, and then what we'd say after that.

This is a great start,
I thought to myself.
We've got the basics covered.

Now, what else is here?
I could see that there was another set of questions these ideas raised, disruptive questions, provocative questions. *If this is true, then you'd have to rethink that . . . And if you take that seriously, then the implications for a person's life would be huge . . .* The further I went, the more it opened up. One question led to another. One insight pointed to another discovery. This connected to that.

That's the thing about a sacred text: You read it, and then it reads you. Like a mirror. You're reading a story this

person told or a letter that person wrote and suddenly it's
not about them, it's about you. It's showing you possibilities
you hadn't considered, a shadow you didn't know was there,
something to encounter that you'd been oblivious to. I could
feel a momentum building, like these ideas were taking me
somewhere unexpected and compelling.

Ed started to stack his notes in a pile.
Well, this one is ready to go, he said.

Wait.
What?
We're done preparing?

He was right.
He knew our audience, he knew where they were, he knew
what would help them. And the work we'd done, it was
good. That sermon would connect with people, I could see
that.
So yes, he was right.
This one was ready to go.

But I was just getting started.

This teaching had so much more right here just under
the surface. So many more questions, provocations,
implications . . .

I sat there in that office within an office,
knowing that he was right,

that this one was ready to go,
and also knowing that I wasn't done.
That I had to keep going,
had to keep exploring,
had to take it further.
I was thinking about that sermon,
but I was thinking about my life.

We come from tribes.
These tribes we come from share common assumptions
about how the world works, how life is to be lived.
Families, schools, sports, neighborhoods, towns. Work,
religion, politics, worldview. There's a safety and security
in the tribe, the sense of belonging you feel, the rituals
that ground and center you with these people in this place.
There are the rules that keep things running smoothly,
the codes and unspoken agreements that keep everybody
in alignment, the rewards that recognize your efforts
and keep you motivated. There are the tribal leaders and
authority figures who remind you what matters and what
doesn't.

**And then there are those moments when something rises
up within you. An itch, an ache, an idea, a restlessness, a
longing for more. A conviction that there is something
else for you and it's not *here*. You can ignore it, deny
it, pretend like it isn't there. But to do that is to let
something within you die.**

Why do some keep going and others stay where they are?
Why are some content with how it is, while others
have a relentless desire for change and growth and new
experiences?
Why do some settle, and others want more?

Jesus told his students a story about a farmer who's planting
seeds and the seeds fall on different kinds of soil. Some of
the seeds take root and grow while some of the seeds don't.
He doesn't offer any comprehensive explanation for why
some people respond one way and others respond a different
way. It's as if Jesus is saying to his students, *I don't even get
how it works . . .*

It's that feeling you get when you run into someone you
knew years ago and you start talking and within minutes
you realize that they're still telling the same stories, still
seeing the world like they did way back when. You're jolted
into this realization that you kept going, and they *stayed.*

You heard something,
and then you followed it.

Sometimes it's a small voice,
or a whisper,
or a series of events that seem to insist they're related to one
another,
or there's a question that won't go away,
or an anguish that refuses to subside,

or you feel like you're suffocating,
or it's a desire that only gets stronger,
or you can't pretend that you believe any of it anymore,
or it's this sense that something within you has expanded
and you don't fit like you used to,
or this knowledge that a chapter has come to an end,
or this truth that for you to be you, you have to keep going . . .

It can be terrifying,
and lonely,
not knowing what's next,
or what the costs will be,
or how you're going to figure it out,
or how you're going to pay the bills.
It can also be electrifying,
for the very same reasons.

That job with Ed was a dream gig. He had been such
a master of a mentor, me following him around and
constantly asking him questions.
What a gift he gave me.
But I couldn't stay.
I had to keep going.
I told Ed a little while later that I was leaving to start a new
church.
He smiled and said,
It's about time.

*   *   *

The therapist leans in, looks me in the eyes, and says,
You've been running too fast, too hard, for too long.
This is new to me, sitting in a therapist's office, telling him
how lost and numb and exhausted and ashamed and sad I
am. It's the *lost* part that is killing me. I have no idea what
is what, or where to begin. I'll take whatever he's got. I'm
desperate.

It wasn't supposed to go this way.

Kristen and I and some friends had started a church. We
had so many ideas we wanted to try. It felt like a giant art
experiment. A man named Roger said we could rent a
building he'd just built for a dollar a year. We ordered some
stacking chairs so people would have somewhere to sit. My
friend Kent put together a band so there'd be some music. It
had this punk rock, do-it-yourself, bare-bones feel to it. It was
a church, but it felt more like a happening. Or a movement.

And it just kept getting bigger. Thousands and thousands
and thousands of people. Someone gave us an old mall. We
started hiring staff—ten people, then twenty, thirty. Then
seventy-five. An expert somewhere on these kinds of things
declared that it was the fastest-growing church in American
history. Which is a ridiculous thing to claim, or even to keep
track of, but it only added to the surreal sense of what we
were experiencing.

It felt like it had happened overnight.
I had been the intern, the assistant, the new guy in that

previous church, and then I left and within weeks—literally, weeks—I was the *senior* pastor of this new church.
I was twenty-eight.

I'd walk into the office and there would be a large stack of phone messages for me. I'd go to a meeting and leave with a long list of things to do. The service would finish and there'd be a line of people who wanted to talk. I'd go to the grocery store and I'd get stopped by someone who wanted to tell me a story about what they were experiencing in our new church.

It was such a high, being a part of something like that.

I'd been reading about the Jewish world of Jesus and how in the first-century rabbinical system you would become a student of a rabbi, learning to do what you saw the rabbi doing.
A *student*.
That stuck with me.
Learning, growing, expecting to be surprised by whatever was coming next.
Full of questions.
Assuming you had so much to learn.
And for a student in that world, it wasn't just what you knew intellectually, it was how you lived it. How you embodied it. What it looked like when it came to life in your particular flesh and blood and time and place.
This image of a student—hungry, curious, open to new ideas and new ways and new forms, this caught hold of us. It's how we talked about who we were at our new church.

Students.
All those people,
gathering to learn and grow,
the energy was extraordinary.

One Sunday I taught about resurrection as a way of life, a
way of orienting your life around generosity and compassion
and hope. We'd been getting more and more involved with
a microfinance bank project in one of the world's poorest
countries, giving loans to people so they could start their
own small businesses to feed their families and send their
kids to school and build houses. At the end of the sermon
I invited people to give whatever cash or loose change
they had on them to that project as a way of practicing
resurrection. *Let's all together give people on the other side of
the world some literal good news today.* We counted up the
donations after the services and people had given a quarter
million dollars.

That's what it was like.
One astonishing moment after another.
This had all been some ideas rattling around in my head
and heart, and now it was happening. And it was beyond
anything I ever could have imagined.

Everywhere I turned something strange or compelling or
surprising was happening. Or there was some crisis. Or
something wasn't working and people were frustrated. I'd
mention some new program we were starting and the next
morning hundreds of people would call the office to get

involved. Or someone had another story to tell. Or someone was asking for something.

The sheer volume of it all was pulverizing. And all I knew was to say yes. Yes to more commitments, yes to more work, yes to more people. We were growing and expanding—who would ever say no to that?

It was all so thrilling, until it wasn't.

Sheer newness and adrenaline can get you really far down the road. That fuel is very powerful at first. But eventually it runs out, when everything isn't as new as it once was.

I was sitting in that therapist's office because Kristen had found me in my office that evening lying on the floor in the fetal position, unable to do much of anything. Kristen was really scared, so she called the therapist and drove me to see him later that night at his home office.

She told me later that she was thinking that night as she drove, *I wonder if our life as we know it is over.*

That same week the church had celebrated its five-year anniversary.
There were some balloons.
And stories.
And singing.
And people raving about how their lives had been changed through our church.

I was not ready for a celebration.
I was in no state for all that.
I did my best to participate,
but all I kept thinking was,
If this is the cost, it isn't worth it.

I felt like I had been swallowed up by a giant black hole, like
I couldn't see anything, like I couldn't get at why I felt this
way, why I was so dead inside. The therapist's name was Dr.
B., and he listened to me go on for a bit, and then he kindly,
gently, firmly informed me that I was angry.

Me? Angry? No way. That was not me.
I was known for joy.
But he was resolute.
No, you're angry.
It was so shocking to hear that.
And true.
I knew it in my bones.
I was angry.
Really angry.

That's what it was.

It was like there was this door, and it had the word ANGER
written on it, and the only way forward was to open
that door and go into that room. I was terrified. But also
desperate. And in enough pain to try it. So I did. Slowly, and
ever so gradually over the next few sessions with him I was
able to identify the causes of all that anger, some going back

twenty years. I remembered events when authority figures had crushed my spirit.

That's the best way I could describe it. Moments when I'd tried to express something about who I was and I had been shut down. Something central to who I was, some essence, had been tramped on. Like I hadn't been allowed to be me.

And in response, I had stored up reserves of *I'll show you* anger. That's a particular kind of anger. When you feel like someone wouldn't let you be you, it strikes at the core of who you are. And that sacred wound can animate all kinds of action. There's a ton of activating energy there.

It's as if somewhere within me I reacted to those events with *Really? These are the rules? Well, I'm going to leave here someday, and I'm going to go and work so hard that I'll create my own world where I decide what the rules are.*

No wonder I was so driven.
No wonder I pushed myself so hard.
No wonder I had such a hard time saying no.

That one insight led to new questions:
Why am I so good at telling people what they want to hear?
which led to
Why am I so scared of letting people down?
which led to
Why do I move so fast—what is it about this pain that I'm driven to stay a step ahead of it?

which led to
Why is it so hard for me to say no?

It was like there was a door on the other side of that ANGER
room, and there was something written on that door. And
I could open it and go into that next room. And then there
was a door in that room . . . on and on it went.

Anger,
the need to please,
fear,
ambition,
not being good enough,
it was endless.
In a good way.
And so freeing.

There was an urgency to what I was learning because of the
public dimension of my work. Being in front of so many
people like that brought with it this unnerving sense of
exposure.

I wanted those crowds.
I wanted to be speaking to all those people.
I had so much to say and I was so passionate about it.
I felt like I was made for it.

But also I knew that people were evaluating me, judging
me, rating me, critiquing me, comparing that Sunday to the

Sunday before, deciding if it was good or not. Deciding if I
was good or not.

It was like a really intense heat. Or a blinding spotlight. Or
a magnet. Whatever little shards of metal, no matter how
small or slight they were—
an insecurity, a fear, a vulnerability—
that magnet of being in public like that,
it brought whatever it was to the surface.

I'd wake up on a Monday morning, wondering why I made
a certain comment the day before, wishing I could do it over
again and not say *that*. That joke, that comment, that extra
sentence that was unneeded.

But once I started walking through those doors,
and finding out what was in those rooms,
and experiencing that liberation,
I began to see it all differently.

I could go there,
and I was fine

Those places that most intimidated and frightened me
within myself, I could enter and I'd survive it, whatever it
was. And not just survive it, there was new life in there.

A friend of mine told me about a woman named Sister Virginia,
who did spiritual direction appointments. I didn't know what

spiritual direction was, or what it meant that she was a sister, but my friend insisted that I would get along great with her.

So I made an appointment. I showed up at the Dominican Center where she worked—this was all new to me. It felt like a convent. Or a spiritual teaching center of some sort. And then she walked in and she was probably sixty-five and she was dressed like my aunt Dorothy and she was wearing these sensible black orthopedic shoes that may or may not have had Velcro straps—she explained that she was kind of like a nun in street clothes and she lived in an apartment not far from where we were meeting.

She told me she was from Boston and she talked like it, and then we got right to it. *Why had I made the appointment?* she wanted to know. I started listing my frustrations and things that needed fixing. Quickly it became clear that she had no interest in helping me fix my problems. She just kept coming with the questions.
Why do you think that's a bad thing?
Why is that something that needs to be fixed?
Why do you think that person sets you off like they do?

Her questions started to have this unexpected effect. I saw that what I thought was the issue wasn't the issue. Something else was. Something I hadn't been aware of. Something really surprising.

It was like a hunt,
or a quest.

Instead of all that angst of
Why can't I get this situation to go the way it's supposed to?
it became
Oh, this is interesting, let's see what else is in there . . .

It was like those things I thought were problems somehow
got turned into signs, pointing me to new awareness, new
questions, new possibilities.

How did she do that?

She said her job as a spiritual director was to join me in
whatever I brought to her, watching to see what Spirit was
up to.
Spirit.
I knew that word.
But not like this.

She had this assumption—
this *trust*—
that something else was in that space between us,
something at work in those disruptions I brought to her,
something stirring in all that angst and anxiety.

It was like catching a glimpse of a force, or brushing up
against something that eluded shape or form.
There was something happening in there—
in the problem,
in the mess,
in the confusion—

when I went in there.
Something active,
something alive,
something empowering.
Something very hard to name,
but very real.
Spirit was her word for it.

This was jarring for me because I lived in a world of fairly
clear-cut distinctions—
things were either
good or bad,
there was
success
and there was
failure,
you're either
winning or losing,
things are going well,
or they aren't.

It's *this,*
or
it's *that.*
One
or the
other.

But with Sister Virginia those categories were getting blasted
to pieces. I was discovering something present and active in

all of it,
bringing something new out of
all of it.

I'd come to an appointment with something frustrating I
wanted to talk about, only to learn that that frustration had
something new and good to teach me . . .

This Spirit she spoke of, this power and presence at work
in those encounters included but then transcended those
categories. It was one thing to try to get rid of the angst and
anxiety and problems, it was something else entirely to listen
and see what it had to say and then follow it where it led.

I made a number of appointments with her.
I'd come with a situation to be solved,
and it would somehow turn into an invitation to be
answered.
I'd leave those sessions exhilarated.

It wasn't that my problems were gone,
it's that they weren't the point anymore.

Of course I had to tell people all about what I was learning.
One Sunday I started my teaching by saying,
I go to therapy.
It felt so dangerous and risky to say that.
To *admit* that.
In that time and place, spiritual leaders didn't talk like
that. The job was to give answers, not to publicly talk about

getting guidance. I hadn't grown up in a world where people talked much about these things. Counseling? Therapy? Spiritual direction? That was for people with problems. People who struggled. People who, you know, had issues. People who weren't cutting it.

Going on an inward journey, discovering the *why* behind why I did what I did—this was all new territory. I stood up there on that stage going on and on about how we don't have to live wondering why we respond the way we do in particular situations and why we develop certain patterns and habits or why certain dynamics develop in our relationships or why particular people get under our skin.

It's all connected, I kept repeating.
It's all connected.
Where you come from and who you come from and what you've experienced and how you react to certain events and people and what you think about your failures. You can go in there and figure this stuff out.

Everywhere I'd go people gushed about how successful I was with my new church. I was starting to do interviews, and I was getting invited to speak around the world. I never stopped hearing how incredible it was.
But all that *success* had broken my heart and made me question what success even is.

That's why, months and months later, I stood on that stage going on and on about *spiritual direction* and *doing my interior work and dealing with my issues,* going to great lengths to explain *how everything is connected to everything else.*

There was something childlike about it. Like a kid who just got the best gift ever and has to tell everyone about it. I have no idea if anything I said that day made sense to anyone who was there.

But me, I was more alive than ever.

Around that time, I'm standing in a hallway in the bowels of an arena in Atlanta, Georgia, listening to a man I've just met tell me that his company does sermon research for famous megachurch pastors—he lists several of them—and he'd love to tell me more about how his company could help me.

Sermon research?

That's a thing?

I'm so repulsed and yet fascinated I don't interrupt. He goes on, explaining how he and his staff provide these pastors with ideas and articles and stories and information for their sermons.

What?

This is a business?

He makes money doing this?

I can't believe this exists.

This art form is deeply personal to me, something flowing out of my heart and mind and soul and life, something I've given myself to, putting in the hours, becoming more and more familiar with the nuances and subtleties over the years as I hone the craft, continually learning and stretching and growing . . .

You can pay someone to do that for you?

And those pastors he listed—does he think I'm one of them? Is this a club I'm a part of that I don't remember joining?

And that word.
Megachurch.
I've just recently begun hearing people use it, and it gets under my skin.
When it's used in reference to *me,*
megachurch pastor,
I wince.
I notice how many people I meet stop me after a few minutes of conversation and say, *You're not what I expected.*
What do you mean? I ask them.
Well, you know, you're a megachurch pastor, I thought you'd be more . . . and then they go on to describe the assumptions they had about me.
This happens all the time.

I'm there in the bowels of that arena because I'm speaking at this massive event, and there are a number of megachurch pastors and authors speaking at it as well. What I feel as I walk in among all those leaders and their entourages is that I'm out of place.

It's like its own culture, like I'm visiting a parallel religious world for the day when I speak at this event. It's got its own music and insider language and consultants and celebrities and rules about what can be said and what can't be said.

Soon after that a pastor friend of mine is in town and we get together to catch up, and then he asks me if when we're done I'll drop him off at a meeting he's having with some other pastors. He gives me the address, and when we arrive, I discover it's a private airport. He gets out of my car and goes over to greet these other pastors who are arriving on private jets. I sit there in my Volkswagen, watching them all shake hands from a distance, feeling this profound sense of alienation.

I experience this sense of alienation often, but most acutely when I sit in meetings at our church. I love these people and have great respect for them, and I love the stories that we never stop hearing from the people in our church. It's an honor to be a part of it—that's with me always—this sense of gratitude that I get to be a part of a movement like this, but there's an ache in there as well.
An ache that never goes away.

I sit in meetings, listening to these people I work with wrestle with the challenges of serving all these people who come to our church, and I want to be somewhere else.
This is meaningful work,
and I'm glad they're doing it,
but I have this persistent conviction that it's not my work.

My work is somewhere else.
Something else.

I have ideas of things to make.
Lots of them.
Books, films, teachings, tours—the ideas never stop coming.
Like I have to make them or I'll spontaneously combust. I
sit in those meetings with this voice in my head constantly
repeating,
I just wish I could go do my work.

But for the people I'm sitting in those meetings with, this is
the work. They're exactly where they should be.

I often sit in meetings where the subject of the meeting veers
into what I'm not doing. What I could do better. How people
don't feel like I'm leading them. I become weary of hearing
what I'm not.

One leader tells me, *You have to eat your vegetables.*
That's literally what he says. He goes on to say that it would be
nice if we all lived in fantasy worlds where we could just create
whatever we wanted whenever we wanted to, but in the real
world, we have responsibilities, and it doesn't matter whether
we like it or not. He says I should be sitting in even more
meetings, taking more control, stepping up like a real leader.

Another pastor confronts me about my failures as a leader,
telling me that it's not about my art—he says the word *art*
with an edge in his voice—telling me that my efforts are

misguided, that the only thing I'll do that truly matters in the end is build a bigger, better, more impressive megachurch. I stumble out into the hall after that meeting and lean against the wall, holding my stomach. The dissonance within me is overwhelming. I have this deep, resonant inner voice that keeps insisting that I'm here to make things, but then I'm surrounded by these voices—strong, smart, clear voices—telling me that my primary job is to lead this church that I started.

Somebody asks me what my three-year vision for the church is.
I don't have one.
I pause, thinking about the question for a moment more.
Still nothing.
Blank.
All that comes to mind is the next few teachings, the books I want to write that are rattling around in my head, the next three short films I want to make, this article I read the day before that reminds me of a line from a song that relates to a parable Jesus told that connects to something that happened to me the previous week—all of it slowly starting to come together in me, forming something new. Another book? Another film? Another teaching?

This is what lights me up.
This is what I think about all day long.
This is what I'm here to do.

I'm well aware that people would love to have this job. I'm very tuned in to how fortunate I am. I know exactly what

a gift it all is to have the chance to lead something like
that.

I feel shame.

And supernatural exhaustion.
Carrying around all that anxiety,
day after day after day.
The body knows.
Our bodies always know.
Mine did.
Whatever doesn't get expressed and dealt with gets stored
somewhere in us.
In the bones, the cells, the heart.
I was so tired but unable to sleep well.
I was trying so hard but unable to stay focused.
That sort of thing.

And the questions—shame is a master at those haunting,
relentless inquiries.
Why can't I do it all?
Why can't I be tougher, stronger, more organized, more
strategic?
Why am I unable to be what these people say I should be?
Why do other people seem to be able to do this effortlessly and
I can't take one step without tripping?

Because.
It's not my path.
It's like a whisper,

but it's loud enough to hear.
And it never goes away.

Kristen, as usual, is a step ahead. Sometimes she would say
to me,
What if you were an oil painter?
She goes on,
If you were here to make beautiful and meaningful paintings,
then we'd set up your life to be as simple and focused as
possible so you could do just that.
That helped so much. There was something that sounded
so clean and Zen-like about living with that kind of
clarity.
Something involving *soul*.
That's what she kept talking about,
soul.

We're made of the same stuff as everything else.
Carbon, oxygen, hydrogen, nitrogen—there are these basic
elements that everything is made of, including us. Rocks,
trees, oceans, bodies, stars. Same stuff.

I call it *thingness*, this matter that everything is made of.
You can hold it in your hand, you can feel it, measure it,
make things with it. Wood, stone, skin, bone. Thingness has
form, shape, texture, boundaries.

Take a rock. Any rock. Hold it in your hand. It has weight.
Shape. *Thingness*. It's either in your hand, or it isn't, it's over

there on the coffee table or next to you on the armrest, or it's there on the ground. It has *form*.

When something has form it has edges, boundaries, visible outlines. You can clearly see where it begins and where it ends.

A rock is here,
not there.
Same with your body.
Your body is made of thingness.
Elbows and knees, teeth and hair and blood. We can visually see where your body begins and ends.

But then we also have a pulse. Blood is *flowing* through our veins. Our hearts are *beating*. When we breathe, we *inhale* and *exhale*.

A rock has thingness,
but a rock doesn't do *that*—
Pulsing, flowing, beating, breathing—
That's something else,
something *more*.

Think of a plant.
A plant is made of thingness,
but a plant also has *life*.
It can live, and it can die.
Like a person.
And *life* is significantly more complex than just thingness.

Life has more complexity,
but less form.
Where does a pulse begin and end?
Can you hold breath in your hand?

You can hold a rock in your hand. But life, pulse, flow,
process—that has form, but less specific shape and borders
and form than something like a rock that's made of just
thingness.

We're made of *thingness,*
and we also have *life.*

There's more.
We also have *minds.*

We can think and process and know and analyze. Way more
complex than a rock. Or a plant. The mind can name things
and organize them. The mind creates language to identify
and make connections.

Picture the color blue.

You did it, right?
Wow.
You saw something blue?
You created or remembered or imagined or conjured up a
color?
You did that *in there*?
In your mind?

Or this question:
Which came first, the moon landing or the iPhone?

You answered, right?
How?
You went back in history,
and then you went back even further,
and then you saw the two events in a larger spatial scope of
time and you identified a sequential relationship—
Your mind did that?
Very impressive.

So there's
Thingness,
there's
Life,
there's *Mind.*
There's also, of course,
more.

When I was in sixth grade my homeroom teacher, Joan
Iwasko, told us that we should work hard to get good grades
because when we got to high school our grades would
permanently count on our transcript.
A hush fell over the room.
We had no idea what that meant,
but it sounded serious.
We were properly unnerved.

And then we all got to high school and learned that those
grades were going to be looked at by colleges when they

determined whether or not to accept us. And then we got to
college and learned that we should get good internships so
that when we graduated we could get good jobs. Or maybe
go to even more school.

And then we got that job, and they showed us to our desk
and we learned what was required of us and what we needed
to do to advance and how we'd be evaluated.
And we did it. We threw ourselves into it and we played by
the rules and gave it everything we had.

And then there's this day when we're driving in to work or
sitting in a meeting or lying in bed wide awake in the middle
of the night or filling out another form or standing there
talking to a guy in the bowels of an arena when we feel this
existential thud in our heart as the question arises within us:

What is the point of all of this?

**It's as if from an early age there is always someone
pointing to a ladder and telling us to climb.**
And so we do. Only to find ourselves in a new space with
someone new telling us that
this
is the ladder to climb
here.

And some of us, we got really good at climbing ladders.
Drop us into any situation and we can find the ladder very
quickly.

In some settings it's about loyalty,
in others it's about making money,
in others it's about working the most hours, being the first
in the parking lot in the morning, the last to leave at night,
in others it's about production or efficiency or volume of output,
in others it's about upholding the reputation of the institution,
in others it's about pleasing the right people,
in others it's all about the numbers—
ladders come in all shapes and sizes.

Which brings us to the problem with ladders: Very few of us
ever took a class that taught us how to know,

Is this ladder even leaning up against the right building?

**I see now what that ache was teaching me, sitting in those
meetings, feeling that angst, knowing that I had a path to
walk and it wasn't this. I was learning about soul.**
We're made of thingness,
we have life,
we have minds,
and we also have
soul.

And soul is real,
just as real as your skin and bones.

The mind *thinks,*
the soul *knows.*

You need mind to navigate the path, you need soul to know
whether this is even *the right path*. Soul is tuned in to whether
or not the ladder is leaning against the right building.

Think about a thought: You can't hold it in your hand. You
can't measure it with any sort of actual device. It exists
within you in a totally different way from a bone or a
heartbeat or your elbow.

And yet a thought is real.
An idea can light you up.
Thinking in a new way can change everything.

So different from a rock in that sense.
So much less form. Way fewer boundaries.

But so much bigger and more expansive and potent.

A rock just sits there, but a thought can travel to the other
side of the world.

And a thought does have some form:
You can have a list of thoughts
or a system of thinking.
You can order your thoughts.
You can recall something you said.
You can construct a sentence.

There is form and structure there,
just way less *thingness form* than a rock.

A rock can only be in one place at a time,
but an idea?
An idea can spread.
An idea can take hold.
An idea can go everywhere.

Now, think about the difference between *mind* and
soul.
Can you *order* or *structure* your soul?
Can you have a *progression* of souls?
Is there *systematic* souling?
Can you recall something you *souled*?
Ahhhh. No.
Doesn't work, does it?
You can order your thoughts, have a progression of
thoughts, recall your thoughts. Not so with soul.

Talk about
soul
like you'd talk about
mind
and it's just
off.

We talk about capturing our thoughts on paper.
Try that with soul.
I was capturing my soul . . .

Doesn't work, does it?

Not big enough, or deep enough, or sufficient enough to
capture what we're talking about when we talk about soul.

You feel soul,
you get glimpses of soul,
you connect with soul.

You hear someone giving their opinion and you think,
I agree with some of what they're saying.

But soul?
Do you *agree* with soul?
Not really.
More like you *resonate* with soul.
You listen to soul.
You look for the soul of something.
You're aware of what something is doing to your soul.

That soul singer strikes a chord within us.
We know what she's singing about.
But if someone asks you to state clearly and specifically what
she's singing about . . . a bit harder to do.

You might answer: an ache.
It's difficult to describe the form.

You see what happened there?
Someone asks you to name the form of soul,
and a concrete description eludes language.

You shift to image, picture, metaphor.
I was dying on the inside.
This job is soul-crushing.
He sold his soul.
She's an old soul.

Soul does have some form—
we talk about *our* soul,
someone else's soul,
the soul of a place,
the absence of soul—
there is some semblance of form there,
but way less than those other layers and levels that make
you, *you.*

All of these different dimensions, parts, aspects,
spheres, layers, essence—whatever you call them—they're
all
real
but they have different degrees of
form.

Some are obvious and tangible—you can access them with
your five senses, you can see them with your eyes right in
front of you—
others are more hidden,
more subtle.
But just as real.

A paycheck you can hold in your hand,

a longing exists somewhere else within you.
Both equally real.

We're each a mashup of all these different dimensions,
and the more you see all this happening at once
within you, the better you can see how sometimes
you need a
poet
and sometimes you need a
mechanic
and sometimes you need more
research
and sometimes you need a
song
and sometimes you need
facts
and sometimes you need to
paint it all a different color
and sometimes you need a
ritual
and sometimes you need
pasta
and sometimes you need a
technician
and sometimes you need
silence
and sometimes you need a
geologist
and sometimes you need someone to sit with you and listen
while you get it all out.

You are irreducible. We can talk specifically about your
mind or your body or other parts that make you
you,
but you are such an interrelated whole that everything about
you bleeds into everything else. Everything about you is
connected to everything else about you. To talk about one
dimension of you is to talk about all of you.

We talk about knowing something *in our bones.*
We speak of our blood *boiling.*
We feel a shudder *in our spine.*

Imagine if someone excused physical abuse by saying,
I only hit his body.
Or if someone was accused of sexual assault and said,
All I did was physically touch her.
Or if someone was controlling others through fear and
intimidation and said,
I'm only manipulating their minds.

We recoil against these sorts of defenses because we
intuitively know that our skin and soul are connected.
Our minds and bones are united. Our hearts and blood and
thoughts are entangled.

We're made up of many parts,
and at the same time we're one.

Imagine if someone said,
I only believe in things I can understand.

What?
Your world is only as big as what your mind can
comprehend?
Or if someone said,
I only trust things I can see.
Really?
Reality is limited to physical sight?
That's just one small sliver of all the ways we know
things.
How could a person ever live that limited?
Or what if someone said,
Reason is my only guide?
That sounds, well, quite reasonable,
and reason is absolutely essential,
but if that's your only guide, you'd be cutting yourself off
from most of the ways humans have known things for
thousands of years.

All of these different
layers
dimensions
elements
essences
parts
make you
you.

It's all blended,
integrated,
meshed,

bleeding into one another,
talking to each other.

When someone is speaking and you have this sense that
they're just repeating something they've heard before you
think,
It sounds like they're just going through the motions.
Or
Their heart is not in this.

They're talking and forming sentences and thinking
thoughts—that's mind—but without appearing to be
connected to anything deeper within themselves.
Soul.

Or that feeling you get when you tell someone what they
want to hear but in doing so you violate something within
yourself. A sense you have of who you are, an awareness that
when you aren't true to this sense you know it.
Soul.

Or you pull up to a new strip mall and everything is clean
and shiny and branded within an inch of its life and it's so
perfect that you say,
This place has no soul.

What do you mean by that?
What you mean is that someone drew up a plan and had a
strategy and there were lots of meetings and people were
given directions and they did surveys and crunched the

numbers and analyzed the data and then they went and
found that piece of land and built that building and found
those tenants and put up those signs and made sure there
was plenty of parking—but maybe without anybody ever
asking,
Is this what we want?
Or
Is this good for the world?
Or
Do we care about this?
Or
Are we proud of this?
Or
Is there any of us in this?

That question is huge: *Is there any of us in this?* Because
that's what you're picking up when you pulled in and
said, *This place has no soul.* What you're articulating is
an absence of a self. You didn't feel anybody behind all
that brick and neon and stucco and concrete. You didn't
sense that actual human beings wanted this and gave of
themselves for this to exist. What it feels like is someone
had a job and they were told what to do and they did it.
Mind received its marching orders and mind got the job
done. One of the more obvious ways we notice the presence
and absence of soul is in architecture—buildings tell us all
kinds of truths.

*Mind does things. Builds. Constructs. Achieves. Follows the
plan. Wins whatever there is to win.*

But soul—soul calls to your deepest, truest self.

Sitting in those meetings,
trying to lead that church,
I was surrounded by people telling me what I should be
doing.
Voices and budgets and programs and opinions and
constant comments—that's a lot of form, a lot of tangible,
physical, real pressure giving me constant feedback on who I
was and what I was supposed to be doing and what it looked
like to be successful.

And then there was soul.
This deeper voice within me telling me another truth,
coaxing me to rethink what success even is.
I had my own path,
and it wasn't this,
and what you do with a path is you walk it.
That can sound so simple,
like, you know,
just do it.
But walking your path, when you're surrounded by multiple
voices with strong opinions about what you should be doing,
that takes tremendous spinal fortitude.

My version of an old, old story:
A woman goes on a quest to answer the one most
important question: *Who am I?* She sets out from her
village and she hikes up the nearest mountain because

she's heard there's a wise yogi living up there in a cave. She hikes for a day and comes to the yogi's cave. She enters, she bows, sits down, and asks the yogi, *I'm on a quest to find the answer to the question, Who am I?* The yogi shakes her head and replies, *That is far too profound a question for someone like me, I cannot help you.* So the woman keeps hiking, farther up the mountain. Days later she reaches another cave, entering to find an old saint, hunched over a fire. She sits down and asks, *Can you help me? Who am I?* The saint smiles. *Oh, that is beyond me.* The woman leaves and keeps going higher up the mountain until she is above the tree line and it's cold and windy and after several days she arrives at another cave where she finds an old woman, alone on a rug. She sets down her pack and asks,
Who am I?

The old woman looks her up and down and then arches an eyebrow and smiles as she says,
Who's asking?

I love that story.
Who's asking?
What a question.
I laughed so hard the first time I came across it. I loved it because I was discovering the self behind my self, the question behind the question, the who behind the who.

There's the emotion or the feeling or the thought, and then there's this thing that happens when you step back and

observe yourself having the emotion or feeling or thought.
You discover that you aren't the sum total of the experience
you're having. There's a you that's bigger and beyond that
experience. There's a you that can witness you having that
emotion or feeling or thought.

There's
I'm angry
and then there's
Oh, look, anger.

You step back to see the YOU that's doing the witnessing,
and you get a bigger perspective. But then you can step back
to see the YOU that just got a bigger, better perspective. You
keep stepping back, only to discover there's another
you
behind that
you.

We can't get to the last you behind the you behind the you,
because there will always be another you behind that you.
We are absolutely sure that you exist and yet the deepest,
fullest *you* behind all those other yous we can't access in any
literal, tangible way.

If we ask you who you are, you can answer by telling us
where you were born
or
where you went to school
or

how tall you are
or
who you're related to
or
what you do with your time,
those are all answers.

They do help identify you, at one level.

You could also answer by telling us stories about pain and
loss and difficulties you've encountered. Or you could tell
us about your personality, your temperament, or how you
scored on a psychological evaluation. You could tell us what
sign you are, what Enneagram number you are, what your
spirit animal is.

And yes, those would all help identify you.
But there's more to us.
Thingness, life, mind, soul.
All real, all with different degrees of form.
That story, the one about the woman who gets that answer—
Who's asking?—
that story gave me language for another part of me.
Another dimension to being human.
One way, way beyond form.
Whatever that is,
and however it worked,
I wanted to understand more . . .

* * *

There was this woman in the church named Carol who
I talked with from time to time. She was a literature
professor at a local university. One Sunday morning right
before the service started she pulled me aside and said,
You're a mystic,
and then she gestured toward all the people who were
taking their seats and she added,
And they don't realize it yet.
That moment, it imprinted on my heart.
What a gift she gave me.
Mystic.

I kind of knew what she was saying,
and
I knew *exactly* what she was saying.

The mystic has had the direct experience. The mystic
knows *personally.* The mystic doesn't need an institution
or a system or a dogma to tell them what they have already
experienced. The mystic doesn't need an authority figure to
validate what they know is true.

I was never that interested in religion.
Or that word *Christianity.*
Carol understood that.
I was after an experience . . .

I had been noticing something mysterious happening in my
teachings. Someone would come talk to me afterward and

tell me how what I'd said had helped them make peace with their mother's death or how it helped them forgive their ex or something similarly personal and transformative.

I'd listen and then tell them how grateful I was that they'd had that experience, and then I'd think,
There was nothing in what I was saying about that . . .

But for them, there was.
I would be talking about something like generosity or imagination, and someone would tell me how much it helped them understand addiction. Or loss. Or regret.

Very mysterious, this phenomenon.
And it kept happening.
People having very personal and particular experiences in my speaking that didn't appear to have anything to do with my speaking. At least on the surface.

I noticed that the more present I was in what I was saying, the longer I had lived with what I was saying, the deeper the place it was within me, the more this happened.

I began to see how much these spiritual talks I was giving were like architecture. Instead of building something with wood and stone and brick, I was building spaces with words. And then people would come into those spaces and see and hear and feel all kinds of things. Often way beyond whatever I had seen and felt.

This is true of songs and paintings and nature and events
and classes and programs and all kinds of art and design.
You create something,
and then you share it with others,
and they have their own experience of it,
which may have similarities to why you made it in the first
place,
and may not.

They may have an experience way beyond anything you
ever could have imagined for whatever it is that you've
created.

Something was at work in these talks I was giving—
something that transcended me—something way beyond
the form of spiritual teaching.

Spirit.
That was the word Sister Virginia used to describe that thing
happening in those appointments with her. Something
active and animating, doing something in all those messes
and tensions I would bring her.
Spirit, that was what these people were describing in their
experiences in those teachings I was giving.

Healing,
clarifying,
reconciling,
reorienting,
remembering,

re-centering—
this Spirit wasn't anything you could get your hands on in
any tangible way, and yet it's as real as anything you could
hold in your hands.

Spirit needs form.
That was the giant truth I was feeling my way into.
Spirit needs form,
and form needs Spirit.
That was the other truth I was finding my way into.
Both are needed.

We need forms—guides, reference points, traditions,
lineages, films, sculptures, texts, prayers, poems, stories,
songs, rituals, practices, reminders.

They help us access and experience Spirit.

We're here on earth,
in these bodies,
feeling the pull of gravity,
knowing that we're only here for a while.
But then there are these moments—
like brushes or glimpses—
of love and connection and hope,
and suddenly we're here,
and we're everywhere.
Our feet are on the ground,
but we're flying.

Our hearts are still beating,
but our souls are soaring.

Around this time, Kristen and I were in Italy for a friend's
wedding. The night before the ceremony we were having
dinner in a vineyard, and the host gave us a tour of the
grounds. At one point he led us into a basement storage
room filled with these massive wooden barrels of wine.

After explaining the various steps in the wine-making
process, he launched into an impassioned speech about the
earth and food and abundance and grace and gratitude and
friends and how we all need each other and how generous
the earth is and how holy and sacred all of life is.

It was the best sermon I have ever heard.
Still, to this day. The best.
In that basement,
in among those old barrels.
There it was again,
Spirit.

Think about all of the greatest moments of your life.
Something was lurking there in all that form, wasn't
there? Some life, some voltage, some love, some sense of
connection and hope and openness—
even trying to name it feels like falling short of the power
and depth of the moment.
What you sensed was

Spirit
there in that
form
whatever it was.
People, food, nature, music, sex, birth . . .

I was part of this massive religious machine,
but what I was after was an experience, a feeling, a depth, a
glimpse—
once again,
language fails
I found myself picturing this church we had started like a
front door. And I was inviting people to step through that
door and into a room that has no walls or windows . . .
From the finite into the infinite.
From what you can see and touch to that which exists in
other categories.

Like a song.
You can sing a song.
Or you can lose yourself in a song.

Everywhere I went people wanted to talk about the church—
the stories, the numbers, the programs, the details, the
attention it was getting.
However great some of that was,
I was beginning to see how much of it wasn't the point,
how much of it was actually a distraction from the thing it
all existed to help people experience in the first place.

And that *thing*—
that enlivening, inspiring brush with Spirit—
you don't need any of that religious activity to have that.
Just your breath.
Your heart.
Your openness.
That can happen in silence just as easily as in a room with
thousands of people.

I was conflicted.
Surrounded by all those people,
and all that religion,
and all that good,
trying to help people see the thing behind the thing,
the point behind all those points,
the Spirit in and through and above all that action and talk
and organizing.

Like when you're learning to ride a bike. Whoever is
teaching you tells you to
Keep pedaling
and
Steer
and
Don't hit that mailbox!

At first, those words help.
You're repeating those phrases in your head,
trying to do what they're telling you to do,
riding farther and farther with each try.

And then you get it.
And you're riding the bike.
At which point you aren't repeating those words because
those words have become flesh.
They are no longer external to you,
they've become internal,
they've become embodied.
Their instructions
have now become
your reality.

That was the point all along,
to feel that particular thrill of gliding along with those
wheels spinning under you.
To move beyond the words to the experience of riding a
bike.

As I began to see how my work was creating space
where things happened way beyond me, my
understanding of religion itself began to be radically
transformed.

I'd give a talk about Jesus teaching us to love our enemies
and how if you love your enemy, then they won't be your
enemy anymore. They'll be something else. The act of loving
your enemy dissolves the category of
enemy
with you over here on one side
and
your enemy over there on another side.

To love is to move beyond those categories of
you
and
your enemy
to
both of you, humans.

The form, the teaching, the truth moves you *beyond the form.*
Like there's an arc, or a movement, or a trajectory in
the words. If you take them seriously, they take you
somewhere.
If you do it,
then you'll find yourself in a different place.
If you absorb the words,
they'll become flesh and blood,
and you aren't the same person you were.
If you listen to what they're saying,
pretty soon you'll be riding the bike.

**The last thing Jesus came to do is start another
religion.**

Creating another religion would give human beings another
way to divide ourselves.
Us and them.
This religion
and then
that religion.

There's a great line in the New Testament about Jesus
coming to bring about a *new humanity.*
I love that phrase
new humanity.

The boundaries kept dissolving, as I became more and more
aware of Spirit in and through and around all these vast
and varied forms. Some of them fitting into the category of
religion, most of them not. All of them helping me experience
the deep, powerful spiritual energies present in all of creation.

There was a question that came up often around the church,
the question was:
What do we believe?

At first, I was the loyal soldier, the good son, the faithful
leader, and I tried to answer it. I gave teachings and
messages and talks, I did diagrams, I made charts, I met
with people in smaller discussion groups, all in an attempt
to make it clear *what we believe.*

What I began to see is that it didn't clarify much of
anything. What it did was raise even more questions.
What did I mean by the cosmic Christ?
What was I talking about when I talked about life to the
fullest?
Where did I get that part about nonviolence and empire?
How did I define oppression?
Was I sure caring for the environment was central to faith?

That sort of thing.
The more I tried to define it,
the more I tried to nail it all down,
the more it defied those neat and concise definitions.
Trying to bring clarity,
it turns out,
raised even more questions.

We would have these eucharist services—also called
communion—where we served bread and wine and we'd
all take it together as a shared ritual, reminding us of our
common humanity with everybody, everywhere. We'd
talk about the story of Jesus, whose body is broken and
blood is poured out for the healing of everything. We'd
talk about how we were setting the table for the whole
world, how Jesus comes to tear down the dividing walls
between all of us so we can reclaim our bonds as one
human family. This ritual is very mysterious, because it
challenges whatever labels or systems we've cooked up to
divide ourselves.
People would ask, *Who is this ritual for?*
We'd respond, *Everybody.*
They'd follow up, *Who do you mean by everybody?*
On and on it went.
I'd do a series of teachings being as precise and clear as
possible on who we were and what we were trying to do and
where it came from and how we saw ourselves and what the
beliefs were behind all of it and people would ask,
Yes, that's all great, but what do we believe?

It was maddening at first.

And then it started to get funny.

This was the breakthrough for me, realizing that no matter
how well you got the forms *right*—the language, the
definitions, the explanations—it was still possible to miss
the intention of the form. The forms aren't the goal, the
goal is an experience of Spirit. I began to see that you can
have every form imaginable but without Spirit, without
that animating, propulsive energy doing something in
it, it's just a form. Just a prayer, just a set of beliefs, just a
religion, just words.

I came from a world where the job of the spiritual leader was
to have the last word on things. To explain it. To tell people
what it means. To teach people how to do it.

I was coming to see that my job was to have the first word.
To start the discussion. To set the words in motion, so that
they could do that mysterious thing they do in all of us.

I kept coming back to the beginning of the Bible. The first
book is called Genesis, and Genesis begins with a poem.
Once again,

so obvious,

and so revolutionary.

Because some truths are so beautiful and profound only
poetry is up to the task of describing them. In this poem, the
divine breathes into dust and a human comes into being. I
love the imagery of it—it's just earth, dirt, dust, *but then it's*

breathed into. In the Hebrew language, the original language
of the poem, the word for
breath
and the word for
spirit
are the same word.

We're just a form.
Dust and bones and blood.
But then we've been breathed into.
Spirit.
There's a fundamental dignity inherent to being a human
being. A nobility. A spark. A divine image.
Nothing can extinguish that.

We need forms.
But that's what they are—dust. Dirt. Earth.
It's the breath that gives it life.
That gives *us* life.

We need both, that's what I kept coming back to.
We're surrounded by forms, forms are what make the world.
The invitation is to allow Spirit to transform all these forms,
so that they become everything they can be,
guiding us into fuller experience of the depths of life.

A mystic.
Of course I am.
Aren't we all?

* * *

I'm sitting with a mother and father whose son is an American soldier fighting in Iraq. We're meeting because the previous Sundays I had given a series of teachings protesting the war in Iraq. These parents have lots of questions for me.

They love their son, they love their country, and they don't understand why I would publicly oppose this war. It's an intense conversation, and I'm moved by how open and curious and honest they are.

I know exactly why I'm sitting with them.
Yes, it's because of those teachings.
But there's another reason, flowing from a decision I'd made a few years earlier, and that decision was turning out to be way bigger than I had realized at the time . . .

When I first became a pastor, I was thrilled to meet up with other pastors. There was a bond I had with people who were doing something similar to what I was doing. We'd meet up and talk about what we were learning and the challenges we were facing, and then an astonishing number of times the conversation would veer in a particular direction.

The pastor I was with would start talking about a book he or she was reading and how it was helping them. They'd rave about this book—whatever book it was, whoever wrote it—and how it was answering questions they'd had for a while, how it was giving language to things they'd been feeling.

And then they'd pause, and they'd say something like, *Of course if I told my church I was reading this book, I'd probably be fired.*
I heard endless variations of this, again and again and again in those first years I was a pastor. It wasn't just a conversation, it was a pattern.

These pastors were split.

They had their professional religious persona, the one that kept the donations coming in, repeating the approved doctrines and dogmas, protecting the boundaries and maintaining institutional stability, keeping their job in the process.

And then there was their true self—that hungry, thirsty, curious, learning, and growing self that wanted to be more and more alive.

A few years into our new church I had done a series of teachings on women's equality and how women are free to be whoever they're here to be. This is obvious, and yet for a number of people in our church this was disturbing. A group was so upset with what I had said that they organized themselves and tried to have me removed as the pastor of the church I had just started.

I laughed when I first heard this, and then I was devastated.

I was told they were working to have my ordination papers
revoked. I didn't know what that meant, but I think there was
a piece of paper somewhere from my first job, confirming that
I had in fact answered those questions well enough.
They wanted to take that away?
It was all so surreal. And absurd.
A piece of paper. Revoked?
A doctor in the church confronted me, arguing that
women can't be leaders in the church because they're too
emotional. He stood there in front of me trying to make his
argument, but he kept stumbling over his words *because he
was too emotional.*

I was thirty-one. I hadn't had critics like this before. This
was new.

A few weeks after those teachings I was having lunch with a
pastor whose church had—and still has—a list of things that
women can't do in their church. His church had just issued
a public statement refuting me. There was this moment
while we were eating when he paused, and leaned in, and
then asked me a question about why I had been giving those
particular teachings.

It was the spirit of the question that struck me.
It wasn't accusatory, it was curious.
Like he'd cracked open a door just a bit, and was thinking
about sticking his head in.

And then he immediately changed the subject.

There was this split second when he allowed himself
to entertain a new, more inclusive and expansive and
empowering view of the world—but then he shut down.
Like a window opening briefly, but before any fresh air
can come in, it closes. If he had actually listened, or went
on his own quest, he might have found something that
contradicted the dogma of his church, and he wasn't up for
that conflict.

Around that time Kristen and I were traveling and we visited
a longtime friend who'd recently become one of the many
pastors of a huge church that had just built a fifty-million-
dollar building. He's giving me a tour of the facilities, and
as he shows me the auditorium that seats thousands he tells
me that they need to bring in a quarter million dollars every
week in offerings to keep the church running.

I have a visceral reaction to this number.
I have to steady myself.
I feel like I'm suffocating.
I think of those pastors,
and all that money they have to bring in.

How would you ever grow and change and learn and expand
with those kinds of pressures?

What if one of those pastors told that church,
Hey, I've been rethinking some things . . .

That's not how you keep a quarter million dollars coming in every week. You do that by repeating what everybody already knows. You do that by reassuring the donors that you aren't changing.

It was like these spiritual leaders I was meeting had a Sunday game face they put on to keep their job, and then they would take it off and talk honestly to me about what they were learning and how they were changing and what was really lighting them up.

I knew I couldn't do that.
This was absolutely clear to me.
I couldn't live split.

I would follow it where it leads,
whatever that meant.
Kristen and I talked about this often.
We talked about the costs, the risks, what it might mean.
We didn't know where it would take us.
What we did know was that it was the only way forward.

I had started doing interviews, and this often came up. The interviewer would ask something along the lines of,
You're a spiritual leader, but you seem to keep growing and evolving . . .

The first time it happened I started laughing.
Why is that so funny? she asked.
Because isn't that the point? I said.

Then she laughed. She got it.

I went on, *How broken is the system when that's unusual for a spiritual leader? Isn't that the job—to keep learning, transforming, following it where it leads . . . ?*

I knew there might be more.
Critics, disruptions, that sort of thing.
But I couldn't live split.
I had to follow it where it leads.
And if I eventually had to leave,
I'd still have my integrity.
I'd still have my soul.
And, of course, I could always find some other way to be a spiritual teacher.
I didn't need a piece of paper to do that.

I kept reading the Bible, and it kept reading me.
I was reading the book of Leviticus and learned that one of its major themes is the importance of sustainably caring for the earth.
That's in the Bible?
I then went back to the poem that begins the Bible in the book of Genesis. Yes. It's there as well. This sacred responsibility to care for the earth. In the Bible, having a healthy and sustainable relationship with the earth is not a cause or political agenda, it's an obvious and unavoidable fact about human life. Any healthy spiritual vision for life begins with the awareness that everything is connected to everything else, and that begins with us having a healthy connection with the earth.

I read about the Exile, where this Jewish tribe is taken into captivity and hauled away to a foreign land. It's one of the major stories of the Bible. A group of prophets rose up to explain why this had happened, and one of their main explanations is:

You didn't give the land the rest it needed.

Amazing. The reason given for why their economy and culture and political structures were destroyed was because they didn't live on the land in a sustainable way.

It was endless.
I'd see something new,
I'd follow it,
that would take me somewhere else new,
which would connect with another truth,
and then eventually I would give a teaching on it.

Exile wasn't something I had been familiar with. But I did know that feeling of being far from home. Home can be geographic, but it can also be a state of the heart. You're in the same place you've always been, and yet you feel like you've been displaced. The more I read, the more I could see not just how central exile is to the Bible but how central it is to the human story.

I read more of the prophets, these poets and sages who spoke all kinds of truth to power. Another of the ways they explained why they'd been taken into exile was because there was a widening gap between rich and poor in their society, and whenever that happens, the entire system is in danger of imploding.

Again and again prophets like Amos announce that
if more and more wealth ends up in fewer and fewer hands everybody will suffer.

How had I missed this?
How had so many missed it?
The Bible tells an old, old story about a small group of people and yet you dive into that story and the implications and insights for our world and our time are endless.

The prophets helped me understand the teachings of Jesus. He comes from that same line of prophets who called out the corrosive politics and practices of empire, announcing a new vision for humanity not based on greed and violence but generosity and compassion for the vulnerable.

On and on it went,
all of it coming to life,
showing me that what is political is spiritual—
there is no division—
that how we arrange ourselves as societies and nations naturally flows from deeper spiritual impulses that are sometimes harder to spot but just as real as anything you can see with your eyes.

* * *

**And then President George Bush landed on the deck of
that aircraft carrier, announced that the mission was
accomplished, and quoted a Bible verse.**

That was the day I was radicalized. I'd been slowly tuning in to
the spiritual undercurrents present in all our relations—from
individuals to nations—but some light went on, something
clicked for me when he landed on that aircraft carrier.

The Bible was written by people living in the Middle East
who'd been conquered by one military superpower after
another. The Egyptians, the Babylonians, the Assyrians,
the Romans—this Jewish tribe had been on the receiving
end of a horrific amount of imperial violence time and
time again.

Because of this repeated oppression, the writers of the Bible
are very suspicious of dominating empires. There's a line in
the Psalms about how

some trust in chariots.

That line perfectly summarizes the strong negative
sentiments of the writers of the Bible. The ones who trust in
chariots are the oppressors, the violent, the conquerors who
dominate everyone in their path.

And in the Bible you never stop reading warnings about what
happens when these empires get ahold of weapons. They
can't get enough in their insatiable need to expand. That's the
distorted spiritual energy of empire: It can never get enough.

I saw how the storyteller in the book of Kings wants us
to know that King Solomon is building a temple using
slave labor. These people were slaves in Egypt—that's the
foundational story at the heart of the book of Exodus—
and their God liberated them and then gives them a new
way to be a nation, not oppressing and enslaving others
but always looking out for the widow, the orphan, and
the immigrant. Always looking out for the ones who are
in the place that they once were. *You were oppressed, so
always do what you can to relieve oppression. Like God
did for you.* But they forget the story of their people and
within a few generations they're building a temple to
honor the God who rescues people from slavery using . . .
slaves.

This is a major moment in the Bible.
They've become the new Egypt.
They've forgotten the story of their people.
They're now the oppressors.
This is a dominant story of the Bible—
and it's a very political story,
which means it's a very personal story.

*Be wary of empire building, because the endless accumulating
of wealth and power will destroy your soul.
Don't become indifferent to the suffering of others,
because you'll lose yourself in the process,
leading to more misery for everyone.
Don't ever forget the grace that was shown to you,
don't ever forget the liberation you experienced.*

Always extend it to others,
because in doing so you're keeping your own story alive.

To read these ancient texts carefully is to find ourselves in them. That's what inevitably happens. You read it, and then it reads you.

I was beginning to see why this particular tradition had been so dangerous and disruptive over the years.
History is usually told by the winners, the victorious ones who tell stories about how they won with the help of their gods.
But the Bible.
the Bible is different.
It's a series of poems and stories told by people who have been conquered again and again. Instead of going on and on about their greatness, these writers are masters of self-critique. Their heroes are flawed, their stories brutally honest, their leaders shown for who they are. Solomon is an arms dealer, he's the new Pharaoh, and he's building another Egypt. King David is a man of blood. On and on it goes, with warning after warning against the greed and indifference of empire that carves the world up to give more and more to a few while everybody else has less and less.

I began to feel like I'd been let in on a conspiracy.
How did this book lose its power and poignancy for so many?
How did spiritual leaders manage to make it so boring?
How did it become for so many something other than a full-fledged manifesto for a new and better world?

I was thrilled to see that this ancient collection of poems and letters and stories is more revolutionary and dangerous than anybody realizes . . .

It's about food and land and economic practices that benefit everybody. Justice is the dominant theme, which is about everybody having enough. There's a passage at the end of the book of Leviticus that commands everybody to forgive every single debt every seven years so that everybody everywhere can have a fresh start. The entire society gets a clean slate every seven years.

There's another command in Leviticus that when you're harvesting your crop leave a corner of the field for the orphan, the widow, and the immigrant so that everybody—especially those who have arrived from some other place—can have enough to eat.

These are radical ideas about how to arrange a society, and they're laid out in great detail in books thousands and thousands of years old. Reading these ancient texts, I couldn't help but see how much they had to say about the American empire in the world with its insatiable need for expansion and its chariots and F-14s and aircraft carriers and drone strikes. America is the largest arms dealer in the history of the world.
America has enough nuclear bombs to blow up the world *multiple times.*
America is the only nation in the history of the world to drop a nuclear bomb on another nation.

America did it twice.

And now America leads the charge to decide who gets nuclear bombs and who doesn't.

America has around eight hundred military bases around the world. Britain, France, and Russia have about thirty military bases outside of their borders combined.

America is about 5% of the world's population and has around 40% of its weapons.

Recently America dropped 26,171 bombs in one year. When Americans gather and sing our national anthem, there's a line in it about *bombs bursting in air.* The glorification of weaponry and violence is baked into our origin song. This massive American economic engine that reaches to the ends of the earth was built on the backs of slaves. Even the discovery of America wasn't a discovery. There were already people here. Who were systematically massacred and marginalized in the endless, insatiable thirst for more. More land, more wealth, more expansion.

In the Bible, there are those who
trust in chariots.
America.
We're the ones with the chariots.

No wonder so many Americans misread the Bible. If you're a citizen of the most dominant global military superpower the world has ever seen, what do you do with a book that is relentlessly critical of dominant military superpowers?

You either ignore it,
or you take it seriously,
or you turn it into nice parables about the human heart,
or you make it about what happens when we die or the
world ends in some other time, in some other place.

That's what happened for many to the book of Revelation,
the last book of the Bible. It's actually a letter, written
from a pastor in political exile to his church. They're
living under a suffocating empire. He writes to them in a
particular genre of political poetry, trying to help them
see the spiritual forces at work whenever empire builds
a head of steam, crushing everybody in its path. He's
writing to open their eyes to the depth of the experience
they're having, helping them see the larger forces at work.
He's not writing to them about some day thousands of
years in the future when the world might end, he's writing
to real people in a real situation, giving them clarity and
courage and hope to stay true to another way of being
human.

That's how the Jesus movement began, in resistance to
the dominant Roman Empire of the day. Those first Jesus
followers knew exactly what they were doing, articulating
a new way to be human, free from the endless cycles of
violence and oppression that have held people down for
centuries.

So when the president of the United States of America, the
most dominant military superpower the world has ever

seen, landed on an aircraft carrier and announced military victory over a Middle Eastern nation, I saw this event as another chapter in an old, old story about the corrosive effects of empire.

And then the president quoted from the book of Isaiah. Of all books, that book.
Isaiah.
Isaiah was a prophet who wrote to his people in exile, giving them a vision of the future when they'd be liberated from the empire that had conquered and oppressed them.
He gave them a forceful and imaginative vision of a new day when people would take their swords and beat them into plowshares, so they could cultivate the land, free from bloodshed as they built a better world of peace and justice.

And now the American president was quoting that text of all texts on the deck of an aircraft carrier to celebrate a military victory.

As I watched the footage of that speech,
I was furious. And also conflicted.
About more than just that speech and that war.
About that word *Christian*.
I'd struggled with that word for years. I'd met so many people who called themselves Christians who didn't seem anything like Jesus, and I'd met so many people who would never use that word Christian to describe themselves, and yet they showed me in so many ways what the way of Jesus looks like.

As a label, it just didn't work that well.

And then there was this whole culture that had built up around that world. Books and music and movies and programs and networks and organizations. So much of it so lame. Like it was a word that got tacked on to things so that people could gloss over how safe and mediocre and impotent it all was.

I had chafed for years against that word.

Sometimes I would stop using it.

Then I would use it, but with a string of disclaimers and adjectives so people would be clear what exactly I meant and what I didn't by using that word.

Which was exhausting.

And awkward.

But this, this was different.

This was historic, systemic, and wrong on a much deeper level than just words and adjectives.

There was this massive Christian religious subculture that claimed the president as one of their own, had helped elect and then reelect him, and was relentless and unquestioning in their support of a profoundly unjust war that was going to cause untold suffering for generations. These people claimed they took the Bible seriously, but they had fallen for that ancient seduction we've seen again and again.

Empire.

They were deeply enmeshed, actively propping up the very thing Jesus came to set people free from.

In the Bible, that's not the way of Christ.
That's called *anti-Christ*.

The war in Iraq, and the unquestioning support of it by
people claiming to be Jesus followers, revealed a spiritual
bankruptcy at the heart of the dominant Christian culture
in America.

I often thought of walking away from the whole thing.
That was tempting.
Stop giving teachings about Jesus, stop reading the Bible,
stop pretending like there was any good left in that tradition.
But I couldn't.
There's too much truth, too much power, too much
wisdom in this ancient movement to walk away from it
just because the American religious/military machine had
lost its way.

**I didn't have to walk away from what has shaped and
vitalized my life in a thousand ways because somebody
somewhere bastardized and blasphemed it.**

I could double down on it.

I had to say something.
I had to give those teachings.
I had to show people that this giant monolith that claimed
to be the Christian voice in the world had gone off the rails.
I was just a pastor in my early thirties in the Midwest,
but I had a bellyful of fire.

I stood up there giving those teachings,
trembling,
so convinced that this war was going to haunt the world for
years to come . . .

Toward the end of that meeting with those parents
whose son was fighting in Iraq the father said something
very telling. He was talking about the people of Iraq, and
how they needed liberating, and wondering if America
would be held responsible if we didn't go over there and
fight that war and remove their leader. He was worried
that we had all these tanks and planes and weapons and
if we didn't use them to defeat evil dictators, we'd be
judged for it.

Ahhhhhhhhhhhhh, I thought, *there it is.*
There's the problem.
Right there.
I was thinking of the writings of Isaiah.
Isaiah reflects the thinking of a number of those
revolutionary Jewish prophets who insisted that

**the real crisis at the heart of humanity is a lack of
imagination.**

There are these ruts, these ways people have been doing
things for thousands of years that keep us stuck in the
same old cycles of violence and revenge. What is needed is
imagination to break us out. New ideas, new visions, new
solutions to free us from the same old enslavements.

That's what I saw in that father's concern. An assumption—
so deeply held that it was unquestioned—that change—
regime change, political change, liberation—can only
happen through coercive military action. Through
violence.

This is the myth of redemptive violence.
It's been around forever.
It's the belief that when someone wrongs you, the way to
make it better is to wrong them.
They bomb us, then we bomb them.
Which never, ever makes things better.
What the myth of redemptive violence does is keep the
violence in circulation. Back and forth the violence goes,
without anybody ever learning anything.
That's the heart of it, right there.
A lack of learning.
A lack of new thinking.
A lack of imagination.
There's no other way to change the world?

This is the revolutionary truth at the heart of the Jesus
story. He's executed for insisting that there are other ways to
change the world.
Love.
Solidarity.
Generosity.
Compassion.
Praying for your enemies.
That's been the power of the teachings of Jesus for

two thousand years. He insists that violence can end. We
don't have to live like this.

We can stop the revenge and bloodshed and all those responses
that never do anything but keep all that pain in circulation.
There are other forces at work in the world, more enduring
and powerful.

**To insist that this is just how it is, is to fail to see that the
great invitation of being human is to change how it is.**
To keep declaring that this is how the world works is to miss
out on the joy that comes from believing that things change
when people decide that the world can work in other ways.

When I crashed and went to therapy,
it felt like an invitation.
Like I was being invited to follow that anger and pain and
angst wherever it took me, trusting that I'd learn and grow
and be better because of it.

I was now beginning to see an invitation for all of us to
think about the world in a whole new way.
It broke my heart, watching people stuck in the same old
patterns of violence and domination.
I was told often that my teachings about love and nonviolence
were nice, but they weren't how the real world works.
I would smile and say,
What do you mean by the real world?
Because isn't that ours to create?

Don't we get a say in what the real world even is?
Who says we can't make something new?

It's all connected.
Small movements over here can cause massive shifts over
there.
Who knows the power we have to tilt things in new and
better directions?

That's what this ancient tradition I came from was doing to
me, it was opening up all these new possibilities, challenging
the dominant thinking of the world around me.

Showing me how powerless all those chariots and bombs are
in the end, showing me how love really does win.
I was becoming radicalized,
and I was just getting started.

I started going to a boxing gym.
I had heard about this retired professional fighter named
Frank Perez Jr., who had a boxing club downtown. It was
upstairs from an auto body shop. You had to climb these
creaky narrow back stairs to get to it. There was a poster
of Muhammad Ali on one wall, with that quote from him
about how he was so fast, when he turned the light off at
night he was in bed before the room got dark.

There was a phrase written on another wall:
The more you sweat, the less you bleed.

I'd show up around sunrise and Frank would be there in his matching sweat suit, ready to go. Frank used the expression *old-school* without irony. He'd have me jump rope, then hit the body bag, then push-ups, then the speed bag, sometimes he'd run a string diagonally across the ring and have me shadowbox up and under it, back and forth across the ring. When it got particularly brutal and I was gasping for breath he'd smile and say,
Old-school.

I loved that feeling of throwing a punch.
I loved that feeling of getting stronger.
I loved making that early-morning drive,
climbing up those stairs,
putting myself through that.
There was something empowering about it,
something I needed at that time.

I was sitting in a meeting one day when the woman sitting to my left slid a stack of papers over to me. I glanced down and started reading from the top sheet.

It was a paragraph about me.
And it wasn't good.
It was mean. Really mean.
Whoever wrote this paragraph did not like me.
There was a paragraph below it.
I read that one.
It was even meaner.
That one was personal.

It was about my kids.
What are these?
I kept scanning.
Ohhhhh, so that's it. They're book reviews.
The woman sitting next to me had cut and pasted negative
reviews from the internet about my first book that had just
been released.

A number of the reviews didn't mention the book at
all. They just went on and on about me. About how
dangerous I am, how I don't get it. How I'm leading
people astray.

I get a little dizzy.
My brain is racing to understand it,
my body feels numb.

I want to address every single specific thing that's written in
every single one of these reviews.
I want to ignore them all.
I want to see if there's anything I can learn from them.
I want to meet every single one of these people and win
them over in person.
I want to start throwing punches.

I am all over the place.
All these different responses sit side by side within me.

I slowly find my equilibrium.
I go back through the reviews.

I notice again that only a few of them actually mention the
book.

I see now,
years later,
what was happening in me.
Something was dying.
Something that needed to die.
A view, a belief, an understanding—
a *misunderstanding*—
whatever it was,
it was dying.

Somewhere along the way I had picked up the belief that my
job was to get people from where they
are
to where they
should be.
From one place
to
another, better place.
From A to B.
From *here* to *there.*

I remember thinking that if I could just get people more—
and there was always a new word to put in that space after
that word *more*—
more open or creative or compassionate or fearless or
urban or globally conscious or environmentally aware or
committed to the mission or—

the word was constantly changing—
but the impulse was the same.
Help people move from where they
are
to where they
should be.

I loved the work I was doing.
It brought me so much joy.
But this other impulse was lurking in there as well, this
belief that it was my job to make this particular change, this
movement, this transformation happen. When you wish
someone were in some other place, and when you see it as
your job to set them straight or open them up or help them
get it, there's a weight that comes with that. It's draining.

The assumption, of course, is that I was in that other, next,
better place. That I got it. That I was ahead. That my job was
to turn the lights on so that other people could then get it
like me.

Why don't they see it? you ask yourself.
They don't have to be miserable,
they could listen to me,
and then they'd be happier and more enlightened.
Why don't they get it? you wonder.
You know, like I do.
There are so many flaws here,
but behind all of them is the delusion that we can change
people.

That's what those reviews were doing to me,
they were teaching me about my limits.

We can't control the outcomes of our work.
We don't get to decide how people will respond to us.
An astonishing amount of the effect of our efforts is out of
our hands.

At first, of course, I assumed it was me.
If I were just more persuasive, more informed, more
articulate. If I took this even more seriously, if I were more
disciplined, stronger, if I were in better shape . . .

We come up against our powerlessness and often our first
response is
If I were just more powerful . . .

But this isn't an obstacle we power through,
it's a truth we make peace with.
I was starting to learn that . . .

And then I discovered atoms.
Curiosity is a great mystery, why some things grab us and
others don't. And quantum physics, it grabbed me. And
helped that thing in me that needed to die, die.

First, it was atoms.
Because everything is made of atoms.
I'd heard this before. Science class and all that.

But until you're ready for something, it's just words. Facts.
Ideas. Stuff teachers are saying.
It's not *personal.*

Atoms, it turns out, are small.
One atom is less than two-billionths of an inch in
diameter.
An atom is smaller than a golf ball in the same way a golf
ball is smaller than *the earth.*
A single grain of sand contains a million trillion atoms.
A half million atoms are as wide as one human hair.
That small.

Atoms, I learned, are made of even smaller things called
particles.
Particles are a lot smaller.
And very, very odd.

There are particles that come into existence, and then they
disappear.
They're here and then they're not here.
And we don't know where they came from, and we don't
know where they go.
Some particles go in and out of existence in
0.000000000000000000000001 seconds.

A particle is the most fundamental building block of the
universe that we know of, and what we now know is that
they exist and then they don't, and we don't know why or
how or where.

At this point I'm a thirty-five-year-old pastor, with
a family and responsibilities and all that, and every
moment I can I'm devouring books on quantum theory
and particle physics. Just inhaling as much as
possible.

Everything is made of atoms,
and atoms are made of particles,
and particles are tiny bits and pieces of energy that come
and go and disappear and appear, billions and billions of
times a second.

So far scientists have identified over 150 different
particles.

So far.

Electrons,
protons,
neutrons,
bosons,
muons,
gluons,
up quarks and down quarks,
bottom quarks and top quarks,
mesons,
pions,
leptons,
the list goes on, because new particles are still being
identified. The smaller we go, the farther in, the farther

down—however you picture it—the more we learn that
the most basic elements that bond to form everything we
know to be everything can be endlessly split and taken
apart.

Everything is made of atoms,
and atoms are made of particles,
and particles are swirling bits of energy and possibility that
never stop moving.

They're small,
and they're also fast.

A single electron can do 47,000 laps around a four-mile
tunnel in a second.
That fast.

There are particles call *neutrinos* that come from the sun.
About fifty trillion of them pass through you
every second.
That fast.

But it isn't just that particles are constantly moving quickly,
it's how they move.

Some particles disappear at point
A
and then reappear at point
B
without traveling the distance in between.

And it isn't just the speed and size and inexplicable ways that they move, it's their unpredictability.

You're standing there next to your car and you look in the window and see your reflection. Sound familiar? Of course. Particles from the sun are hitting the window and some are passing through the glass, but others aren't passing through because they bounced off the glass. That's how you can see yourself. Fairly straightforward.

But why did some particles go through and some bounce back?
We don't know.
We can predict,
there are probabilities
and you can do a lot with those probabilities—
but there's an unpredictability baked into the whole thing.
Some do and some don't.

I had never done well in science. I remember studying for Ms. Hapkiewicz's chemistry test my sophomore year of high school and not understanding a thing. I was intimidated. And bored. It all seemed so flat and lifeless to my narrow mind. Formulas and calculations, numbers. There was so much there I missed.

But this—atoms, particles—this was science?
Because this was thrilling.
It rang true.

That's the best way I can describe how it felt.
It rang true.
Like I'd sensed it all along.

The chair you're sitting in,
the car you're driving,
the clothes you're wearing,
they're all made of atoms.
And atoms are relationships of energy.

Thingness, it turns out, isn't all it appears to be.
This was the revolutionary truth for me,
the one that broke it all open.

**Thingness—the solid, material reality that you can
depend on because you can hold it and see it and feel it—
thingness and stuff and matter are, in the end,
relationships of energy.**

What appears to be solid is not, ultimately, all that solid.

The world, the universe, each of us, all of it—
one big, unending series of relationships?
This is so utterly basic to science,
but to me, it was earth-shattering.

No wonder I had sensed an energy in the soil and water and
air in those places where I came from.
No wonder I had always felt a pulse, a flow, a connection.

No wonder it had all felt alive to me from way back when I was young.

I would sit there wading through one quantum physics book after another, making connection after connection, feeling like a whole new world was opening up.

So much of it reminded me of the Bible. In that Genesis poem there's an energy pulsing through all of creation.
A communal, relational, animating energy.
The word for God in the poem is the word *Elohim* in the Hebrew language, which is a *plural* word.
God is *plural* in the poem.
God—another term for that is *ultimate reality*—is like a community of love.
God, Spirit, Word—all connected, relating to each other, a flow running in and through everything.
Trinity is the word for this communal nature of God.
There's a trinitarian flow humming in everything.
And in this Genesis poem the poet wants us to know that human beings reflect this communal energy.
Of course we do.
We crave connection with each other and everything.
We're miserable without it.
We can't help but make things.
We never stop talking and singing about love.
Poets thousands of years ago were picking up on what scientists are now telling us. What we thought for so long was hard, fixed, material stuff made of thingness is, at its core, *relational*.

No wonder all that systematic theology was interesting for a bit, but it also felt so lifeless.

No wonder I felt such dissonance all those times when people wanted me to state black-and-white, clear, and certain statements about what I believed, as if that were the highest form of truth. As if that's what we're here to do. As if that's the goal.

The whole thing is relationships,
and what you do in relationships is
you enter in.

On and on, my learning continued.

Some particles are bonded together, and then they separate, and then after they separate they demonstrate an awareness of what the other particle is doing without any communication between them.

This is called *entanglement.*

They were once together,
and now they're not,
but they're still keeping tabs on each other,
without any communication between them.
What?

The *Whats?* just kept coming.

When we take apart the things that make this world you and I know to be home, it gets weirder and weirder the further you go in. Again and again I read scientists who insist that if you're studying quantum physics and you're not shocked, you're not studying quantum physics.

Everything is made of atoms, and atoms are made of
particles, and particles are bits and pieces of energy that
move in ways we have no categories for . . .

When a particle travels, it appears to take
every possible path to get where it's going.
Until it's observed.
Then it reveals which path it took.

I'll type that again,
but it won't make it any less strange.
A particle takes all the possible paths at once until it's
watched, and then it reveals which path it actually
traveled.

So strange.
The act of observation forces the particle to choose one of
endless possibilities.
Viewing the particle changes its motion.
Measuring the particle alters what it does.
Seeing the particle affects which course it takes.

I was raised in a modern world that taught me a particular
view of things based on subjects and objects: There's a fixed,
set world, *out there,* doing what it does,
and then there are our thoughts and observations and
insights that exist independent of all that.

You observe it.
You measure it.

You take notes.
You notice.
You view.

It's going to do what it's going to do,
and you can be here or not,
witness it or not,
study or note or learn or observe—
or not.

There's the subject,
and the object,
and a clear difference between the two.

There's a line,
and you're over here watching,
and the thing you're watching is over there doing whatever
it's going to do,
on the other side of the line.

But we now know that there is no line.
There is no out there *out there.*
To witness it is to affect it.
There's only this one reality, and in it everything is
connected to everything else.

This reminded me of an ancient Jewish prayer called the
Shema. It's in the book of Deuteronomy, and it has this line
about how the divine is
one.

The Hebrew word for *one* there is the word *echad,*
which is a oneness made up of multiple parts.
Like a unified community.

All divisions take place within a unity.
All parts exist within wholes.
All wholes form one whole.
Everything that appears to have nothing to do with
everything else is, in the end, connected to everything else.

All that weirdness and strangeness and connection that I
had felt for as long as I could remember was, in some hard-
to-explain way, real.
True.
The world is way more relational, more interactive, and
more connected than anybody ever told me.

I had intuitively sensed it,
but now that feeling was being given language.
What a gift.

Take apart an atom and you discover it's made of
particles, and when you observe those particles you
discover that your observation of those particles affects
what they do.

There's a phrase we use when we aren't going to participate,
we say,
I'll just sit this one out.

But the truth is
Nobody is sitting this one out.

No one is just
seeing what happens.
Seeing
shapes what happens.

**It's a participatory phenomenon,
this universe we call home.**

We all belong,
we're all a part of it,
we're all *already participating.*
We always have been.

This took me back to what I had always believed about the
gospel announcement that everyone is loved and everyone
belongs and there's nothing anyone can do to earn what we
already have.

I thought of all the hours and energy I'd spent
wondering if I was good enough, if I belonged, if I had
a part to play.
I saw all of that for what it was—
unnecessary.
The starting point is belonging.
It always has been.

My life, my work, all these people I was speaking to, all that I was learning about atoms and particles—it was all running together, blending and mixing and creating something new.

I had heard stories about an Irish priest named Father Jack for years.
I'd been told that people came to him for guidance, and he helped them find their way. He seemed to be off the grid, like you had to know someone who knew someone who knew someone to meet him. He was more like a rumor or a legend to me than an actual person.

But then I met a guy who said he knew him—
Father Jack is real?
I was so thrilled.
Father Jack exists?
The fella who knew him gave me his email address, and I wrote Father Jack, asking him if we could have lunch.
He wrote back,
Yes, if you'll sign my copy of your book.
What a response.
Turns out, he lived in Dublin.
I booked a flight.

I was desperate for help.

We meet up and we're taking a walk through this rose garden in Dublin and he quickly figures out that I'd flown there to meet him for lunch and he starts asking why and I start in on how I felt so much weight. How I was tired of the responsibility of trying to help all these people move from one place to another. I went on and on. I must have sounded like I thought I was such a big deal.

When we take ourselves too seriously it gets in the way of the thing that we are so seriously trying to do.

After a bit he stops me.
He's so kind, and so firm.
And so fierce.

He tells me that I have a gift to give, so I should give it.
He says that it's a generous gift that we each give to the world, and we should take good care of ourselves.
To give a generous gift, we must be generous with ourselves.
And to give generously, we must become very good at receiving generously.

Something like that.
I remember looking around at all those roses, jet-lagged and depleted, and feeling this serene sense of release.

It's a gift?
That's what it is?
God, that one word opened up a whole new world.
That word *gift* somehow said something to me about how connected I am with all those atoms and particles, coming and going and swirling in their frenetic glory. And that took me up those stairs to that boxing club to that desire to get

stronger. Better. Faster. Which circled back to those book reviews and my powerlessness over how people responded to me. Which brought me to my lack of control over the outcomes of what I was trying to do.

Give the gift,
and surrender the rest.

That's all that's left to do.
Give the gift.
And enjoy giving the gift.
That I *could* control.
That was the part that got me.
I can control *that*.
It's not about pushing myself even harder,
or being even more convincing,
or getting in even better shape,
or throwing an even stronger punch.

That was all so heavy.
I'd tried it that way.
What a burden.
All that seriousness, all that self-importance, all that belief that it was my job to get people from one place to another.
If the only answer ever to anything is
You really need to do more and try harder
your heart will eventually wear out. Along with your body.
And your soul.

* ➤ *

You won't have anything left to give to whatever it is you've given yourself to.

Sometimes I would stand on a stage with a microphone in my hand, looking out at all of those people and I would feel like my heart couldn't bear it. I could feel the collective weight of all those dreams and scars and burns and loves.

Like it's an actual thing,
hovering there in the room,
this weight.
I could feel it in my bones,
what everybody's carrying around with them.

And I'd want to help.
Every single one of them.
I'd imagine myself whispering in every single person's ear,
You're loved.
You always have been.
It's good that you're here.
We need you.
You're not alone.
You're going to be fine.

On some days I'd interact with so many people, hear so many stories, be exposed to so many people's pain, that I'd feel at the end of the day like it was attached to me. Like they'd handed me something and now I was carrying it around.

These experiences were wearing me down.
I was doing everything I could to help as many people as
possible, and I was learning that something about it wasn't
sustainable.

But I couldn't get at that something.
I couldn't quite name it or get my mind around it.
And then Father Jack said,
Gift.
And my heart said,

Yes.

Your power is important.
You claim it. You use it. You exert it.
You rise up in your power and you give yourself to the ones
you love and whatever it is you're here to do.
But then you learn that power has limits.
That's that truth I was feeling my way into.
And when you get to the outer edges of your power,
you meet your powerlessness.
That's where I was.
And that's what was happening in that rose
garden.
I was being given a new vision of how it all works.

You start with the gift of it all, you begin with the wonder
and awe that you're even here and alive and breathing and
you even get to do this.

That's the starting place.
You always come back to that.
It's all a gift.
You receive it,
and then you give what you can.

You embrace your impotence, your powerlessness, your lack of
control over the outcomes—you make peace with all that you
can't do, with your limits, with all the people you can't help.

Giving the gift is reward enough.
That's where the life is.
That's where the joy is.

And then, on top of that, every result, every bit of progress,
even one person responding favorably to the gift you're
giving becomes an astonishing thrill.
It was such a gift that you're even here and you got to give
yourself to that, whatever it is, whoever they are.
And then it actually helped?
Someone appreciated it?
Someone was inspired?
You got a good result?
Amazing.
It's like stacking grace on top of grace on top of grace.

Father Jack and I talked for the rest of the day, and
he continued to be kind and generous and ruthlessly
honest, and what kept coming back to me was that one word
gift.

Receiving, and then passing it along.
Opening up to power and force and energy way beyond me,
letting it move through me.

I felt this new life surging up within me.
I don't need people to be anywhere else.
I can meet everybody where they are. With love.
I'll give the biggest gift I can give.

I could do *that*.
That sounds fun.
And slightly absurd.
Which reminded me of all those atoms I'd been
learning about that were teaching me how weird the
world is.
We're on a ball of rock hurtling through space?
Our bodies replace themselves every few years?
Everything that appears solid is ultimately a series of
relationships of energy involving atoms, which are mostly
empty space?
Particles come in and out of existence and we don't really
know where they go or where they come from?
We're each made of atoms that used to be other things and
other people, and those atoms will leave us and go on to be
other things and other people?
And this is happening all the time?

I could feel a lightness welling up within me.
Like gravity had less effect than it had before.
Like a weight had been taken off.

Like the divine was winking at me,
like I was gradually being let in on the joke . . .

I started to read those Jesus stories again through a
new lens. He tells a story about people showing up to
work in a vineyard at different times of the day but then
at the end of the day everybody gets paid the same
amount.

What an odd story.
Which is his point.
It's like the story is asking,
Do you get it yet?
Of course it isn't fair.

Since when was fairness the ultimate goal?

The parable isn't an instruction manual on how to properly
run a vineyard,
it's a parable about how your heart works.

Grace isn't fair.
Love isn't fair.
Joy isn't fair.
They exist in other categories.

These phenomena at the heart of the human experience
that fill us with joy and meaning and love were never about
fairness.
Or making sense.

Or how serious you could be.
Or how well you could prove your worth.
Or what you could accomplish.
Or what you could get people to do.

The workers all get paid the same because you can't divide
the infinite. I started to see what all those yogis and
Buddhas and monks and nuns and sages and gurus across
the ages were smiling about.

This experience we're all having here,
this event we were born into—
it's profoundly, deeply, fundamentally *off*.
Odd.
Strange.
Entangled.
Connected.
It doesn't follow any of the rules we thought were the rules
for how it works. A particle disappears in one place and then
appears in another place without traveling the distance in
between.

It's like the whole thing is winking at us.

And the ones who move us,
inspire us,
spur us on,
they're in on the joke.

That's how they're able to help us like they do,
they've made peace with how absurd it all is.

They don't take themselves too seriously,
which is why they have such a serious effect on us.

They smile.
They walk through a rose garden fierce with the conviction
that it's all about giving the most generous gift you can.
They're the ones who aren't here to prove anything because
proving was never the point.
They're the ones who don't need to win because that was
never the game in the first place.
They're the ones who truly disrupt.
They're the dangerous ones.

I'd been living with that weight of trying to wake people up
to the dangers of the American empire and the earth-care
crisis we are in and the need for all of us to go on our inner
journey to deal with our issues—
I'd carried that burden.
I'd talked with a straight face about how I was here to change
the world. I'd read those reviews and wished I could just go out
and win every single one of them over one by one by one by one.

And it was so incredibly exhausting.
Exhilarating, and meaningful.
But absolutely exhausting.
Those issues are more urgent than ever.
I believed in their importance more than ever.
And now I was coming to see there are others ways to share
these convictions,
other energies to engage,

other ways to do my part,
Other ways to coax the whole thing forward . . .

It was this word. *Gift.*
Atoms and particles,
spinning and swirling,
keeping it all in motion.
It's all an absurd, over-the-top, ridiculous gift.
To be here.
I was beginning to see how many truths can only be
communicated though parables and poems and surreal
stories that don't make sense but your heart knows are true
in some very-hard-to-describe way.
I was starting to feel like I was in on the joke.
I was starting to feel like the whole thing is an endless
invitation.
And you say yes.
Again and again and again.
And then you invite others to say yes with you.

**It's April of 2011, and I'm with Kristen at a party in New
York when this man walks up and starts talking to us.
He's charming and kind, and he asks me lots of questions.
There's something about him that's familiar. But I can't
quite place him.**
And I *love* talking to him. It's like meeting a friend you've
had for years for the first time.
And then I catch his name again.
Carlton.

Ahhhhhh, yes. I know who this is.
Carlton Cuse.
He had made the television show *Lost*.
That Carlton Cuse.
It's his curiosity that I can't get over.
It's wonderful.
And so contagious.
Like he's a master *and* a student.
At the same time.

It was a bit strange for Kristen and me to be at that party, partly because the previous several months had been a whirlwind unlike anything we'd ever encountered.

I had written a book that was released two months earlier. It was my fifth book, so we'd done this before, but this book, this book was different.

I'd shown early drafts of the book to a few friends as I was working on it, and they had strong reactions. My friend Mark and I were eating burritos when he said,
This book is going to change everything—everything in your life will be before and after this book comes out.

I didn't know what to do with that.

Another friend, Zach, was visiting from Arizona and I read a bit of the opening chapter to him out loud. He kept shaking his head while I read, repeating the phrase,
Wrecking ball, wrecking ball,

under his breath.

What do you mean by wrecking ball? I asked him.

He smiled and said, *This book is going to be so disruptive.*

Kristen, of course, was way ahead, as usual.

She repeatedly said,

People are going to talk about this book.

And then, on a Saturday night in February, two months
before the book was scheduled to be released, my friend Dan
texted me to say that I was trending on Twitter.

This was new.

We'd made a short trailer for the book,

and it had been posted by someone earlier than planned,

and people had opinions.

About the trailer.

About the book.

A book they hadn't read.

The publisher moved up the release date,

I started doing interviews,

and off we went.

Planes and hotels and book signings and more interviews.

And that word *controversy.*

Everywhere I went that word came up,

over and over.

*The controversy. Dealing with the controversy. Did you see
this controversy coming?*

No, I guess I didn't.

I was slandered, banned, boycotted. All the usual venom
when religious people are defending their gods.

That wasn't new. Or very interesting to me.

What was interesting to me was how out of place I felt.

Like wearing a sweater that doesn't fit.

I was thrilled to hear story after story of how the book was setting people free, confirming suspicions they'd held for years.

That part was incredible.

But it also felt like all that controversy was telling me something.

About who I am.

And what I'm here to do.

Spirit is often lurking in whatever it is you most dislike.

I'd learned that years earlier with Sister Virginia. Time and time again I had sat with her, citing my repulsion toward this person and my frustration with that situation and my animosity toward this event. And then we'd go in there together and I'd see that something new was waiting to be birthed out of all that stress and tension.

I was developing the musculature, bit by bit by bit, to lean in instead of away. To listen, when my first instinct was to plug my ears. To open up, when I wanted to shut down.

So when I never stopped hearing from people that this book I'd written was causing controversy, I found myself listening in new ways, assuming all that noise was there to teach me something new.

When we were leaving that party Carlton gave me his card and told me to get ahold of him if I ever needed anything.

So I did.

I'd written a novel and I sent it to him, asking him if he thought it could be a television show, knowing that he probably got a thousand of these sorts of requests every day. He sent me back a link to an article titled "No, I Will Not Read Your Fucking Script."

I laughed so hard when I read that.

But then he emailed again soon after that, telling me that he had read my novel, and yes, there might be something there . . .

As the energy gradually began to subside around the release of the book, the leaders of the church had a question for Kristen and me. We were close to a number of them, and we trusted them—we'd been through so much together over the years. They told us how much they loved us and loved having us in the church, and because of that they wanted to know what we saw ourselves doing next. Was there another book like that one coming? We talked on and off for several weeks about how the book had taken a significant amount of energy from the people who ran the church and if this was going to be an ongoing occurrence, they needed to be better prepared in the future.

What's next?

The question was so simple.

But it unexpectedly got under our skin. In a good way. And it wouldn't let us go.

What do we want to do next?

Carlton and I continued to explore making a television show together, a show that was gradually having nothing to do with that novel I had originally sent him. I wrote up character descriptions, plot summaries, character arcs. I hadn't ever done anything like that. I'd send another email back to him, laughing at how bizarre it was to be pretending like I knew what I was doing.

One Sunday about a month after that party there was a baptism service at the church. I was greeting people and celebrating with everybody, taking it all in. At one point in the service, I started to cry. And I couldn't stop. Full-on blubbering. Some sort of valve had been opened in me. It was like a torrent of emotion that seemed to have no end.

I kept looking around, wondering if people could tell I was *in the middle of something.*

What is this?

Normally, if I was in that room on Sunday with all those people, I would have been on the stage, speaking, which required a tremendous amount of energy and focus. I'd been doing that in that space for twelve years. But this Sunday was different. I was in that room, with all of those people, but I wasn't up on that stage, I was walking around

and hugging people and seeing this whole thing we'd
created in a new way.

Like I could see it from above.
Like an aerial view.
Like when your kids grow up just a little, and suddenly you
see them and your life together with new eyes.

I kept feeling these words—
that description doesn't do the experience justice.
It was words,
but it was like my body was hearing them.
The words were
There's a church here.
Which I already knew.
We'd been doing this for a while.
The sensation, though, it got stronger and stronger.
There's a church here.
Almost like
Don't you get it?
That's what got me.
Like it was a decisive announcement.
You set out to start a church. You did it.

That's what it felt like.
Like an end.
But a good end.
Like we'd set out to do something and we'd done it and now
it was time to do the next thing.

*   *   *

Endings are often bad. Painful. Awkward. Ugly.
Endings can also be good.
Have you ever stayed too long somewhere—
A job? A relationship? A place?
When we stay too long,
what could have been a
graduation
can easily become a
divorce.

There was a window when it was time to leave,
but we stayed,
usually because it was comfortable,
or familiar,
or easy,
or there was a guaranteed paycheck,
or we were scared of what people would say if we left.

And if we stay past that window,
often things sour.
They turn in on themselves.
It gets toxic.
We lose our joy.

Not all endings are bad.
Some are good. And necessary.
Nothing is wrong, and yet it's time to go.

For exactly that reason.
Because it's good.

This can be a foreign idea if your endings have only ever
been bad. Sometimes you have to leave
because it's good.

Our ancestors were far more tuned in to the natural
rhythms of the earth. There was the planting season, and
then the harvesting season. Summer, then fall, then winter,
then spring. One season starts, and then it ends, and then
another one starts, and then it ends.

The sun sets, the day ends, and you go to sleep,
the sun rises, the day begins, and you wake up.

You eat certain foods at certain times of the year because
those foods are in season.

Today, we can buy tomatoes in a snowstorm in February at
3:00 in the morning. We don't know where they were grown,
or who grew them, or whether they're in season or not. We
want to make salsa in the middle of the night and we don't
ask a lot of questions about where these tomatoes came
from.

This is good, and not so good.

We have more technologies, luxuries, and options than our
ancestors, but with that has come less and less connection

with the earth, with the seasons, with the rhythms of
creation, with beginnings and endings.

**These rhythms reinforce the truth for us year after year
after year that things begin and then they end and it's all a
natural part of things.**

Sometimes it's over,
and it's time to leave,
not because it's bad
but simply because it's time.

I continued creating that television show with Carlton,
eventually going to Los Angeles that summer to spend a
week with him, breaking down the first episode. We sat
in a room and worked every day all day. I was learning
so much, sitting there with a master storyteller. It was all
new, creating a story like that, and yet it was strangely
familiar.

I found myself thinking again and again,
I've been doing something very similar to this for a while now.

A sermon, in many ways, is a story.
There's conflict. And questions. And things to overcome.
And an arc.
We go somewhere, together.
We're surprised along the way.
We aren't the same people we were when we arrive at the
end.

I knew about stories.

We all do.

We grow up with them.

We tell them.

We read them and watch them.

We're surrounded by them all our lives.

But this, this was different.

This experience of creating a story with Carlton was causing a tectonic shift in how I saw the world and how I saw my future. I'd been trained to tell stories as examples of truths. Stories were understood to be illustrations of whatever the concept or principle or idea was.

I had seen this with my book that had recently come out. So many of those interviews I had been doing were about the concepts, the arguments, the intellectual battles that go on with religious people when they're defending their gods. Head games. Hairsplitting. Terms and definitions and labels.

I found myself again and again trying to draw the discussion back to the stories we tell.

Because some stories are better than others.

Stories about a God who tortures people forever in hell shouldn't be told. They're terrible stories. They make people miserable. They make people want to kill themselves. Stories that insist that a few human beings are going to

be okay and every other human being ever is doomed for
eternity are horrible stories.

But stories that fill us with wonder and awe,
stories that remind us of who we truly are,
stories that tell the truth about the mess we've made of
things and how we can turn things around,
these are stories we need more of . . .

Sitting there with Carlton,
I was coming to see that what I had been doing for years was
telling a story.
About who we are.
And what we're doing here.
And how it's all connected.
And where it's all headed.

I was starting to see the story *as* the truth.
The mystery is born in bodies.
The words take on flesh and blood.
The infinite becomes present in histories.
Your history.
My history.
The universal needs the particular.
Spirit needs form in time and space.

Carlton and I,
we could take that story we were creating anywhere.
This is obvious—

because that's what you do when you make up a story—
but also earth-shattering for me.

This truth started bleeding into the rest of my life, exposing
something I hadn't seen before.
Something that took me back to those meetings Kristen and
I were having with those church leaders.
They had asked us, *What's next?*
And for years,
we had had an answer for that question.
What's next is we're here doing the next thing . . .
Something along those lines.

But suddenly,
that response didn't work for us anymore.
Specifically that part about
here.

There was something hidden in that word
here,
something subtle and significant—
an assumption.

An assumption that we'd stay *here.*

We had been giving the same answer for so long it had
become embedded in our thinking.
We're here.
We're not leaving.
This is the story.

A belief—so nuanced as to be almost imperceptible—that
this is just how it is.

And suddenly we saw it.
We can change how it is.

And once you see,
you can't unsee.

**Spirit often exposes the assumptions we've been living
with that we haven't been aware of.**
Sometimes we've accepted rules and codes and limits
without realizing it.
And then Spirit blows in,
and exposes those assumptions,
showing us how limited we've been,
what we haven't seen.
We see what we don't have to accept,
how we can make new rules.

**Spirit often reveals the ways in which we have ever so
subtly submitted to the belief that this is just how
it is.**
Spirit refuses to accept that this is just how it is, because
spirit is inherently creative.

Spirit shows us new possibilities.
About how it works.
About what we have the power to change.

What if this wasn't how it is?
What if we changed it?
What if we decided to do something else?

Kristen and I didn't see it coming.
And then *bang,*
there it was.

We were walking the dog,
not long after that baptism service,
when one of us said to the other,
It's time to go, isn't it?
And the other said,
Yes, it is.
And the other said,
California?
And the other said,
Of course, that's what I was thinking.

That's where we'd started our life together.
That had always felt like home to us.
That's where the new life was.

It's November of 2012, and I've flown across the
country to speak at an event and I'm standing on the
stage doing my thing and it isn't going well. I am
bombing.
I cannot find my groove. I feel like I'm trying to dance to
music that I can't hear.

I've been given forty-five minutes to talk, and around the twenty-five-minute mark I realize that I'm coming to the end of what I had prepared to say. I have no idea where to go from here. I look at the audience, they look back at me. They have no idea what's going on in my head. My mind races, searching for the next thing to say. Nothing comes to mind. A low-grade panic sets in.

I pause, and then I say,
Does anybody have a question?

This is not something that would have happened in my previous life. I was *always, always, always* prepared. Over-prepared. Super-prepared. I'd have way more to say than whatever time I had to say it in.

To add to the angst,
I'm wearing a suit,
standing there on that stage,
running out of things to say.
That's the thought that has been running through my head the entire talk.
Why are you wearing a suit?
And under the suit,
I'm wearing a sweater.
That just wasn't a sartorial move I was used to making.

I was wearing that getup because I was trying to figure out who I was in this new life I found myself in. And sometimes you just don't know what to wear.

I use these phrases *my previous life* and *this new life* because that's what it felt like. Like we'd left one life and we were creating a new one.

And this new one, it was taking a while.

It had been a year since we left the church and our life in Michigan and moved to California. The kids started new schools, we found a place to live, we figured out where the grocery store was. We got California driver's licenses. I was writing a book and leading workshops and retreats.

What a thrill to be starting over like that.
It was also disorienting.
And unnerving.
The unknown often is.

And at times, awkward.

I'd be at a party and someone would ask what I do for a living. I would pause, aware that I could say anything.
Sometimes I answered,
I'm kind of like a consultant.
Other times I'd say,
I'm writing a book.
At least once I said,
I'm working on some ideas.
Sometimes I could laugh about my answers,
other times they left me with a low level of dread.

In my previous life, I didn't go anywhere in public without
being recognized.
And now, I was anonymous.
Sometimes people talk about the fantasy of starting their life
over in a new place where nobody really knows them. We
were experiencing that.
I loved it.

There was this guy named Paul that I would see around
town. One day he said,
I thought you were retired.

Retired?
We had a three-year-old.

I felt like we were just getting started.
Like we were cocking it all up all over again.
Like everything before this had been just a
beginning.

We were so happy.
We'd been in one place.
And then we'd left.
Places can be geographic. They can also be emotional.
Intellectual. Cultural. Tribal.
Or it's your job.
Or your neighborhood.
Or the role you play in a family system.
Or a worldview.

And when you leave,
you find yourself in the unknown.

There's a story in the book of Genesis about a man named
Abraham who leaves his father's household. *Your father's
household* in the ancient Near East was an entire way of
life. Economics, family, authority, worldview, gods—where
you get your food. Leaving *that* was leaving the known
and heading into the unknown. From something that's
established to something that doesn't exist yet.

Strange, how the writer doesn't explain why Abraham leaves
other than saying he hears a divine voice. Something
intimate
and
infinite
is calling to him,
and he listens.

There's this line:
Then Abraham went.

It's such a short line, so easy to skip over.
But absolutely massive.
Because people didn't do that at that time.
The widespread understanding was that history is like an
endless cycle, and what happened to your parents' parents
then happened to your parents and would eventually happen
to you. Everything is some version of a repeat of what came
before.

This story then,
the one about Abraham leaving,
is revolutionary.
It's a step forward in human consciousness.
You can step out of the cycle?
You can leave?
And head into the unknown?
You can step into something that hasn't happened yet,
that doesn't exist yet?
What an incredible new idea.

And the writer doesn't give us any explanation why.
Abraham heard,
and then he went.
He heard something?
That's the best the writer can do?
That's so vague.
Ambiguous.
Fuzzy.

Exactly.
Sometimes the most powerful truths in a story are
the ones that are never explicitly stated. This story has
endured because it's true to how it works. Something
rises up within you, something internal, some force,
some voice, some compelling urge to go. You get some
shape, a little texture, a glimpse of what direction to
head in. You get just enough so you can take the next
step, but not enough to take the risk and faith and fear out
of it.

I knew I had new things to create.
I knew there were new spaces to do my work in.
I knew that there was a whole world of people like me more
spiritually hungry than ever.
But beyond that,
it was the unknown.

There's another story in the Bible about a woman named
Ruth. Ruth is from Moab, and when her husband dies and
her mother-in-law, Naomi, decides to return to her homeland,
Ruth insists on going with her. Why would she do that? If she
leaves her home and goes with Naomi she'll be a foreigner,
with no rights, no land, no resources, nothing to protect her
from the endless dangers of the world at that time.
And yet she insists on going.
Into the unknown.
And once again, the storyteller has no interest in telling us why.
No attempt is made to explain to us why this woman would
want to put herself at risk like this. We don't get any information
about what's going on inside of her. Only a passionate and
resolute vow to follow Naomi every step of the way.

We find this same absence of explanation across a massive
number of stories and cultures and time periods. Something
within us knows it's time to head into the unknown, and so
we do.
It's very, very mysterious,
these forces that work within us.

I was feeling those forces.

We knew there was more,
we knew there was another chapter,
but to leave that previous chapter,
and move into the unknown meant living in the in-between.
Another word for the in-between is *liminal space*.
Liminal is from the Latin word for *threshold*.
You're leaving one room,
but you aren't yet in the next room,
you're crossing the threshold.
For a period of time, you're in neither of those rooms.

Liminal space can be so brutal, and so good.
We leave,
we let go,
we see things we didn't see before,
we listen.

I constantly had to tell myself to be patient.
I would often ask Kristen to remind me to be patient.
That part was unnerving. We create these identities around
our roles and titles and job descriptions and achievements.
They give our lives shape and form and meaning and
definition. Ever so gradually over time our understanding
of ourselves gets shaped by what we do and what we've
done. We cling, we grasp, we hold tightly to these
identities.

And then we find ourselves without them.
Sometimes because we chose to leave them behind,
other times they're taken away without our consent.

I felt so exposed.
So vulnerable.

I remember my friend Chris telling me that people were
asking him,
What happened to Rob?
As in
Where'd he go?
as in
Is he doing anything?

I remember feeling this low-level dread when he told
me that. Like a cold shudder. One harmless comment
from a friend, and my imagination ran wild with endless
ruminations on how to set the record straight and let those
people know that I was still in the game.

That's the thing about liminal space: You're really tender.
Raw. Susceptible to those old forces and fears.

I didn't have regret,
I was flirting with something far more powerful:
fear.
Fear that it appeared like I didn't have any idea what I was
doing.
Fear that it looked like I couldn't hack it, so I left.
Fear that people thought I was somebody, and then I'd
thrown it away.
And here's the killer one:

Fear that I appeared to be done.

I'd take a few breaths,
and tell myself the story all over again—
that this is how it works,
that this is all part of it,
that I come from a long line of people who set out for the
unknown, following it wherever it leads and whatever the
costs—
and I'd feel this surge of calm reminding me that there's
nowhere I'd rather be,
that we chose this,
that we knew we'd be in liminal space,
maybe for a long time,
standing on the threshold,
not in one room or the other,
and that was okay,
because this is where the life is.

Standing there in that suit, I finish what I had prepared to
say to those people, and then ask if anybody has a question.
A few people do. The talk ends, and I walk down the back
hall to the green room.

I sit in a chair.
There's food on a table in the corner.
I'm not hungry.
My sweater itches.
A few people come and go,

telling me they appreciated my talk.
One man says,
Refreshing, as usual.
I barely hear them.
What am I doing?
I ask myself.

I don't feel any closer to a new life,
I feel further.
Like I've taken a few steps back.
I'd been doing this for twenty years,
why does this feel so unfamiliar?
On and on the chatter goes in my mind.
I can't do it the old way,
and I don't yet know what the new way is.
Even those categories of
old way
and
new way
feel stilted and forced.

That's the thing about liminal space.
You're often a little jumpy. A little jittery.
You make things bigger than they are.

I sit there in that chair,
replaying that disastrous talk,
reminding myself,
This is all part of it,
this is all part of it,
this is all part of it.

I had asked for this.
To be taken apart.
To be laid bare.

I knew there was more.
I knew I wasn't done.
And apparently this was all part of it.
It was such a gift,
to be stripped and humbled like that.
Who am I?
We know the answer to that question:
Who's asking?
That's what was happening to me.
I'd lost so many of the identities I had forged over the years,
which was moving me closer and closer to the me behind
the me behind the me. To the me who literally didn't know
what to say when people asked me what I did.
When so much gets left behind,
you discover that you're fine.
You've got a little fear,
like a fly buzzing around your head,
but you're fine.
You're also free.
What a gift.

**Elizabeth Gilbert and I are sitting side by side on a small
stage in an arena parking lot, taking questions from the
audience. Someone asks a particularly heavy personal
question, and there's a pause, Liz turns to me, and says,**

Well, Pastor Rob, what do you have to say about that?
She laughs.
The crowd laughs.
I laugh.
I find myself suspended in one of those split-second
moments that lasts within you way, way longer than just a
split second.
Did she just call me Pastor Rob?
I haven't been called that in years.
I left all that behind,
in my previous life.

We're in this parking lot on this stage because Liz and I had
been invited to go on tour with Oprah. And when Oprah
invites you to go on tour, you say yes. We were speaking in
arenas around the country, and after the first stop Liz and I
asked the organizers for some way to get closer to the people
who were coming, some way to connect beyond standing on
that massive stage in those massive rooms.

And so we're sitting on these stools, and there are mics being
passed through the crowd that has gathered in the parking
lot during the lunch break, and Liz and I are having so much
fun. There's an alchemy between us, some childlike magic
mojo, like we've been doing similar things for years and then
we just met up and compared notes and now it's game on.

And then she calls me *Pastor Rob.*
It's jarring.
And unexpectedly healing.

It knocks something loose within me.

**We craft these identities, and then we cling to them,
grasping them for the sense of security they give us.
And then we let them go, and new identities form,
sometimes around who we**
are
and sometimes around who we
aren't.
I was
that,
but now I'm
not that.

The mind loves this, it can ruminate on these distinctions
all day.
I was that, now I'm this,
They're with them,
She's one of those,
He talks like they do,
I used to be one of them,
What are you?
On and on it goes.

It's that thing that happens when you play a song you love
for somebody and as soon as the song starts playing they
start talking, trying to figure out what other bands they
think this band you're playing them sounds like.

Ahhhhh—it's maddening.

You just want them to stop talking and listen to the song.

You played them the song in the hope that they would enter
into it with you, not stand at a distance trying to name it or
categorize it or even describe it.
You can do that later.

To have the fullness of the experience,
to be fully caught up in it,
is to be present in it.
Not standing at a distance,
analyzing it,
trying to figure out what it reminds you of,
or who it sounds like,
or what label to give it.

Soul doesn't care what it is or what it should be called.
Soul just wants to enter into it.
And feel it.
And absorb it.
And experience it.
Soul wants to participate.

I had left something,
something that had given me an identity,
and I had set out to find the next thing . . .

Pastor, not a pastor anymore.
Church, not church.
That previous life, this new life.

And Liz, she doesn't care about any of those distinctions.

What a gift she gives me. On that day in that parking lot,
pastor is the word for me. That's what I was doing. This thin
slice of an eternal moment breaks me, showing me a path to
embracing all of it.
What I was before that.
What I was in that moment.
Where I'd been, what I'd done.
All the various Robs over all the previous years.

You see me like that?
Fine.
You're going to put that on me?
Okay.
Me being that helps?
Great.

Soul doesn't need to decide whether you're
this
or
that.

I'm all of it.
What I was,
What I am.
All of it.

There's a book I've read many times about the artist Robert
Irwin. It's my favorite book. The book is called

Seeing Is Forgetting the Name of the Thing One Sees.

What a title.

Seeing Is Forgetting the Name of the Thing One Sees.

The first time someone told me about that book, I felt that title in my bones. *Yes, that's it.*

I was more alive than ever.
I was having more fun than ever,
more filled with wonder and awe than ever.
Titles, achievements, what to call myself, what to say when I was asked what I do—I could feel those attachments losing their power over me.
I was gradually forgetting the name of what I was seeing . . .

My understanding of God was tied up in all of this.
It always is.
Because the universal and ultimate is always personal, isn't it?
The question
What kind of universe do you think we're living in?
is a very intimate question.
How we understand the big things is always driven by our most personal struggles and desires.

I was being set free from the idea that there was ever any point to this other than full-bodied participation in the moment we're in.

There's a story in the Bible where Moses asks God what
God's name is, and God answers
I AM.

Moses wants to locate God,
and what Moses gets is
Everywhere.
Moses wants something to wrap his mind around,
and what he gets is
All of it.

What an answer.
Another way you could say
I AM
is
Being Itself.

That's past,
that's present,
that's future.
All of it.
Being Itself, the formless beyond any one form, animating
all forms.
The electricity the entire thing is plugged into.
The water it's all swimming in.

That's every *you* that ever was and ever will be.
All your yous.

The things you're embarrassed about,
the things you moved on from,

the scars you carry with you,
the ways you used to think that you now reject—
we're all of it.

The universe has been expanding for over thirteen billion
years, and we never stop being invited to expand along with it.

I didn't need any distance from where I'd been and what I'd
done in that previous life, it was all with me. It was all part
of me becoming me. I wouldn't be this particular me, here,
now, without it.
You leave,
and you bring it with you.
It's all part of you.

You keep moving,
and you include it all.
You transcend,
and you embrace all of it.

God is less like a noun,
and more like a verb.
I AM.
Being Itself.
The ultimate will always include all of it.
There's a line in the Bible about the God who is
above all and through all and in all.
Just one line,
but so massive.
Above all and through all and in all.

We have painful experiences and regrets and wounds that
make us want to leave
pieces
of our history behind.
This is a totally normal impulse. But it can leave us in
pieces.
Bits here and there, not quite sure what to do with all of it.
Someone mentions a place, and you wince.
Someone mentions a person, and you tense up.
You see a picture from a particular time and you get a pit in
your stomach.
We can easily end up at odds with our own story.
At war with our own history.
Not knowing what to do with certain parts.

But I AM,
Being Itself,
invites us to own every square inch of our story.

I'd left one life,
only to learn it was all with me.
Above all of it and through all of it and in all of it.
What do you have to say about that, Pastor Rob?

**I'm on tour in Australia in early 2016 and I show up at the
theater for sound check and as I walk out on the stage I see
that there's a drop-off at the front of the stage that goes
down twenty or thirty feet, creating this huge gap between
the stage and the front row of seats.**

I walk to the edge and look down to the lowered orchestra pit. I ask the stage manager how long it will be until they raise the pit up to match the rest of the floor height so we can do a proper sound check.

He tells me there's an orchestra that has a rehearsal after my show, and they won't be able to raise it up and then lower it down again in time for their rehearsal so I'll have to do the show like it is.

The gap, I learn, will remain.
I turn to the booking agent, directing my growing rage toward him but realize it's not his fault. How would he have ever known when he booked the show to ask,
Oh, by the way, there won't by any chance be a thirty-foot abyss between Rob and the audience, will there?

I catch myself.
I laugh.
I'm in on the joke.

Did I ever think I'd reach a point where I'd just effortlessly glide—where there wouldn't be awkward interactions and unexpected obstacles and bizarre situations there's no way I could have prepared for?

Standing there on that stage an old familiar force rises up within me, and I can feel all that frustration being converted into joy. I will throw myself into this show even more. I will do everything I can to overcome this *literal* gap and connect

even more with everybody who's coming tonight. I will
watch this unexpected obstacle get turned into a good story,
maybe even for a book someday.

Around this time I go to London to do a workshop. I spend
a significant amount of the day talking about the art of
communicating, giving people practical ways to take their
ideas and give them shape so they can share them with the
world. I'm really, really passionate about this.
I'm there, in London, telling those people everything
I've learned about storytelling and crafting a sentence
and figuring out how to take what's brewing in you and
communicate it with clarity and fire.
We take a break partway through the day. I'm making my
way through the crowd to get something to drink when a
woman stops me and asks,
So, do you have any thoughts on communicating?

Wait.
What?
I just did several hours straight of taking about—
was she even here?
Was she listening?

I stand there speechless.
It's kind of awesome, actually.
She just sat there listening to me for several hours doing
my very best to communicate the importance of good
communicating, and apparently I didn't communicate very
well at all to her what I was trying to communicate.

I laugh.
I feel like someone, somewhere, is winking at me.
Reminding me to hold it all loosely.
To throw myself into it with everything I have,
and also surrender all the outcomes.

I'm speaking at an event shortly after that, and during sound check the sound person asks me what kind of microphone I'd like to use—a headset that I wear on my head that clips around the tops of my ears with a little mic that extends forward, like a motivational speaker or Britney Spears would wear
or
a wireless mic that I hold in my hand?
I answer,
A wireless handheld mic would be great.
The sound person then says,
All right then, but how about you wear the headset mic as well and I'll just keep it turned off and then if the wireless mic fails, all I'll have to do is turn the headset mic on?

Am I being punked?
Is someone filming this?
His suggestion is for me to wear a microphone on my head that won't be turned on?
He's joking, right?

These sorts of strange things have happened to me for a very long time, but I notice as I get further along that I'm less and less frustrated and more and more . . . I think
entertained

is the word for it
as if they contain some subversive joy for me.

Like the rough patches,
the wheels that squeak,
the awkward parts are there to remind me of something,
to keep me loose.
and limber,
and young,
and open,
and present.

I start doing shows at a club near my house called Largo.
Largo is owned by a fantastic Irishman named Flanny who
soon becomes a beloved friend to Kristen and me. Flanny is
very intentional about creating a particular kind of family
setting at Largo. There aren't photos or recordings, so for
a lot of comedians and musicians and artists who perform
there it's this sacred place where we can try out whatever
we're working on at the moment. When Flanny invited me
to start doing shows there I was thrilled.

And so nervous.
As nervous as I've ever been for anything.
I used to give my talks three different times on a Sunday to
three thousand people each time.
Largo, packed out, is fewer than three hundred.
There's something poetic for me in those numbers.
The math here is not lost on me,
I welcome it.

The learning curve starts all over again at Largo.
It's so unfamiliar, trying to figure out how to do what I do in
that space, and yet the first time I stand on that stage I have
this overwhelming feeling:
This was always where it was headed.

I'd set out to see where I could take the sermon—
or to say it another way—
where the sermon would take me,
and here I am.
Exploring more than ever,
learning more than ever,
doing what I can to help people see that everything is
spiritual, you've always belonged, the whole thing is an
endless invitation.

One show I'd feel like everything was clicking, like I'd
found a groove. And then the next show might feel . . . *meh*.
Okay. Fine. A little flat.
What a gift,
to be starting over in a new space like that.
Stumbling along.
Figuring it out.

It's like arriving,
only to start all over again.

I start a podcast.
My son Trace lets me borrow an old microphone he had
stored under his bed.

I set it up at my desk.
It's all new, sitting there in our house, recording myself
speaking, talking to
no one.
Just me in a room, and this hope that what I'm saying might
connect with someone somewhere out there.
I'm used to a crowd,
to bodies,
to the back-and-forth,
the give-and-take,
the exchange of energy.
All that connection between me and the audience,
seeing where it goes,
all of us in it together.

But recording a podcast,
it feels so lifeless.
Like the words leave my mouth and then just drop there in
the air and land with a thud.
Like a bird with no wings.

I keep going.
I make another episode.
I try it slightly differently from the last one.
Week after week.
Episode after episode.
It takes months and months to slowly begin to find my
way.
It's beginner's mind, all over again.

I keep making things,
more things than ever,
more new spaces and places than ever.
The ideas keep coming,
leading me in ways I never could have imagined.
Sometimes it's like gliding across the face of a wave,
other times it's like fumbling around in the dark trying to
find the light switch—other times there's a drop-off at the
front of the stage.
It's so much fun
and
it's frustrating
and
it's thrilling
and
disorienting
and sometimes
I'm more nervous than ever
and other times
I feel like I'm flying.

Sometimes I feel so confident, like I know exactly what this
is and what to do with it, like putting up a shot and while
the ball is still in the air you've already turned your back to
the hoop as you casually jog the other way.
Other times the self-doubt has me in a headlock, and I ask
Kristen to tell me one more time,
It's all going to be fine.
And then she obliges me one more time and smiles as she
says in that velvetlike voice of hers,

It's all going to be fine,
and
I believe it's true all over again.

It's like I'm figuring it out,
but as soon as I do,
something shifts,
and
we get to figure it out all over again.

I resist this endless figuring it all out,
but over time,
it starts to work a kind of magic on me.

We're all endlessly figuring it out.

I realize I've been living for years with the assumption that
at some point you arrive. You get it all nailed down. You sort
it all out. And then from there you get on with it.

But it doesn't work like that.
I AM
is less
noun,
more
verb.
Less a
destination
and more a
direction.

This begins to connect with something I'd read about the origins of the universe, and that reminds me of something from that Genesis poem, which comes together to help me see that I'm just scratching the surface of this truth about how we're all endlessly figuring it out . . .

In the beginning, roughly 13.8 billion years ago, the universe was a single point of infinitely compressed mass.
I'll just keep typing like we all know what that is. We all come from a single point that contained everything that would eventually become everything.

I knew this from science class, like we all do.
But once again, something familiar was becoming unfamiliar, something I'd heard a thousand times was striking me like I was hearing it for the first time.

At first, there was just a single point,
and then there was a bang.

And in the split second after that bang there were only particles. Bits and pieces of swirling, leaping, frenetic energy—that was it.

Nothing else existed,
just those particles.
The universe comes from one
point,

and the first thing it did is become
parts.

It's one,
and then there's a bang,
and then the *one* becomes *parts.*

All those different particles, then,
all those *parts,*
all existed within a whole.
Different particles,
and yet all ultimately united as one.

Belonging is the natural state of the universe.

It splits apart, it divides, it becomes something new,
but everything in that new state still belongs as part of
the one.

**All exclusions have only ever taken place within one
massive inclusion.**

We've all belonged the entire time. Every single attempt
anyone ever made to make anyone else feel like they
didn't belong or weren't a part of it or they weren't worthy
of participating all happened within a larger unity and
belonging.

When you feel excluded,
you're at that very moment *in.*

You've always been in.

You've always belonged.

And then, roughly three minutes into the life of the universe—those particles began to bond with other particles.

Three minutes into the life of the universe, over thirteen billion years ago we know what happened?

Someone figured this out?

God, I love science.

Three minutes in, particles began bonding with other particles. This bonding produced *atoms*.

The universe hadn't seen atoms up until that point. Atoms were new. Particles coming together with other particles created something new that hadn't existed before.

And then, the universe kept going.

Because roughly 300,000 years into the life of the universe, those atoms began to bond with other atoms to form *molecules*.

The universe had never seen molecules before. Molecules were new. Molecules are made of bonded atoms that are made of bonded particles.

And molecules weren't just new, they were bigger and more complex. When particles first bonded with other particles they were joining together to form something bigger and more than themselves—atoms.

Same thing happened with atoms: When atoms bonded with other atoms, they formed something bigger and more complex than themselves, molecules.

Have you ever heard someone say that they're volunteering somewhere or joining a humanitarian organization or leaving their job to go work somewhere else and the reason they give for this is

I just want to be a part of something bigger than myself?

Yes, of course they do.
Everything in the universe does.
Particles come together with particles to join something bigger than themselves called *atoms.*
Same with atoms, molecules—
everything
has a drive to be a part of something bigger than itself, that's how the universe became *a universe.*

A universe that was just getting started. Because at some point 9 billion years into the life of the universe molecules began to bond with other molecules, and that formed *cells.*

The universe had never seen cells before. Cells were new.

This is a pattern. Something bonded with something like it, and that introduced something new, something more complex, something that previously didn't exist. Something the universe had never seen before.

All because of a drive.
A drive to bond, to unite, to come together.

Where does this drive come from?
It comes from within.

This power/drive/force/movement/engine/motion that
has kept the universe moving forward for 13 billion years,
causing things to unite as continually new forms come
into existence, comes from deep within the universe
itself.

It's the most basic nature of reality.
To unite.
To come together.
To make something new.
To seek out new forms and designs.
To move beyond itself.
To keep going.

Have you ever heard someone talking about the meaning of
life and they say,
All that matters are relationships?
Well, yes.
It's even better than that.
Matter *is* relationships.

So when particles bond with particles,
and atoms bond with atoms,
and molecules bond with molecules,
we see something of ourselves there in the earlier stages of
the universe.

We crave coming together and connecting with others because this is what the entire universe has been doing for billions and billions and billions of years.

Connection is an engine of creation.

This is why loneliness creates such a deep ache in our bones. It's holding up—and working against—the direction the universe has been heading for over thirteen billion years. Same with racism. Regardless of where we come from or what we look like, we're all humans, and when humans fail to bond and unite and connect with other humans, that's going against the direction the universe has been going for thirteen billion years.

Which takes us back to cells, that around nine billion years into the life of the universe began bonding with other cells—which of course created something new. New organic structures and new cellular systems and eventually new organisms that the universe had never seen before. On and on it kept going, unfolding, bonding and connecting until we arrived on the scene thirteen billion years in.

There's a direction to what's been happening in the universe.
Like bonds with *like* to form
more,
the whole thing unfolding according to this particular pattern, increasing in complexity and depth this entire time.

There were no atoms,
and then there were atoms.
There were no molecules,
and then there were molecules.
There were no cells,
and then there were cells.
On and on and on,
the whole thing moving forward for thirteen billion years.
It's a dynamic reality,
ceaselessly unfolding,
creating,
moving forward into greater and greater complexity.

Becoming is its natural state.

It isn't what it was yesterday,
and it isn't what it will be tomorrow.

Take a picture,
and you'll have an excellent snapshot of what
was.

And what's true of the universe is true of each of us.
There's a good chance you went to second grade when you
were seven or eight. That first day in that new class you felt
the expanse of that new space. The lessons were a little more
difficult, the math was a little more complex, the vocabulary
words were a little bigger.

Ideally that new class gave you new forms to grow and
expand into. At first they were new, and maybe a little

unnerving, a bit intimidating, but then you settled in. You
learned. You grew. It worked.

For a while.

And then, ideally, you kept going. Kept growing. Kept
expanding. And you came to the end of second grade.
That form helped for a season and then you came to the
end of it and it was time to leave and enter the next form.
Third grade. Which hopefully was just the right amount of
challenge and expanse and bigness and leap.
And then you settled into the third grade.
Until it was time to keep going . . .

Those forms work until they can no longer contain the new
thing that is happening in you, the new expansion that
doesn't fit in the current form.

The same form that can be
liberating and challenging and new and exciting
can become over time
limiting and stifling and conflicting.

A form helps,
until it doesn't.
It liberates,
until it confines.
The problem may not be the form, the problem may be
looking to the form to continue to give you what it could
only give you for that stage. That chapter. That time. That
period of your life.

Second grade was great when you were in second grade.
And then you were done with that form.

Which takes us back to those particles,
leaping and swirling there in those first three minutes of the
universe.
What caused that big bang?
What caused that one to become many?
What caused those particles to begin particling?
Whatever that something was,
it animated particles, which began particling—
and particles are a *form*.
But whatever it is can't be contained by just
particle form,
so it kept going,
animating and energizing those particles to bond with other
particles to create atoms.
A new form.
One the universe had never seen.

In that ancient Genesis poem, this animating energy is
called *Spirit*. And in that poem, Spirit enters and animates
forms, which then create new forms.

Particles couldn't contain the fullness of Spirit,
and that led to something new.
That's what Spirit does,
it brings about new creation.

And what was true thirteen billion years ago
is true now.
For us.

We're all endlessly figuring it out because Spirit keeps doing
something new.
We can fight this,
resist this,
dig in our heels,
wish things were the way they used to be,
or we can embrace it.

We can choose to see it with fear and frustration,
or
we can see it as thrilling and invigorating.

Organizations can keep trying to relive their glory days,
wishing things were like they were when they started.
Nations can get stuck, trying to go back in time, to an
imagined era when things were great.
People can get overwhelmed by nostalgia,
wishing things would go back to how they were.
But the universe only knows one direction.
Forward.
Spirit only knows one kind of creation.
New creation.

It would be easier if someone would just tell us.
Where to go. What's next. What to give our energies to.

What not to give our energies to. Whether to keep at it or drop it and walk away. How exactly to raise this kid. How exactly to raise this other kid who's nothing like that kid. What precisely to say. What to leave unsaid. What exact amount to spend on this, what exact amount to spend on that. When to go, when to stay.

It would be easier if someone would just figure it out for us.
It would take the weight off. We could avoid all those cringeworthy moments and infuriating interactions when we wish we'd known ahead of time and we could have avoided this. We wouldn't have to lie there wide awake in the middle of night repeating all the lines we wish we could have said in the moment.

It would be easier if the universe were a more static place to call home.
If it would just arrive. Or finish. Or cease all this messy becoming. If we could just get it set up once and for all, if we could nail down the forms, if we could just get it fixed. There'd be so much less second-guessing. We'd spend our money better, we'd give our energies to exactly the best things. We'd have no regrets.

Could someone please just show me the map?
That used to be my question. Then I wouldn't have to discern. Then I wouldn't have to make all of these endless decisions that demand I live with the consequences and outcomes. Then Kristen and I wouldn't have to talk so much

about what the next step is, we could just move past all this
endless discernment and decision-making.

It's easy to settle for solid ground.
We see it all the time. Someone is one thing—but now they're
telling us they've seen the light, they're something else—
progressive, *post this* or that, *they didn't get it but now they
do*—but what you sometimes sense is that they are as rigid and
fearful as ever. Like they exchanged one rigid form for another.

It's easy to swap one fundamentalism out for another.

Leaders, teachers, gurus, authority figures, systems,
structures, institutions, codes, movements—they can all
serve very helpful purposes at certain stages. You needed
that, you needed *them*—
the rules,
the teachings,
the slogans,
the plans,
the mantras,
the stories,
the songs,
the doctrines,
the retreats,
the steps,
that wonderful feeling of belonging.

They told you how to do it. They did the discerning with you
or even for you. And it helped give your life shape and form.

They showed you the way. What it looks like when it takes
on flesh and blood. You were one of them. You didn't feel
alone.

Until those forms became traps.
Until you didn't need them anymore.
Not because there was something wrong, necessarily, but
because you kept going.
It's less
right vs. wrong
and more
earlier vs. later
or
then vs. now.

**We spend so much time searching and longing for solid
ground, only to discover it's better than that.**
There's Spirit.
You try this,
you try that.

You throw yourself into it,
and
you hold it loosely.

You give it everything you have
as
you acknowledge that this is what we're doing now,
who knows what will come next?

You're passionate and true to your convictions and
grounded in your integrity
and
you're limber and flexible and open and always
listening.

Spirit never stops
unfolding,
creating,
whispering,
shouting,
inviting us to come along and take another step and enjoy
this.

What do you call this?
This experience we're having,
this source it all flows from,
this sense you have that when someone is violated,
we're all violated,
this awareness you have that everything is connected with
everything else.
A word people have used for thousands of years is
God.
Or *Spirit.*
Or *Source.*
Or *Ultimate.*
Or *That of which nothing greater can be conceived.*
Or *Ground of Being.*
Or *What kind of universe are we living in?*

See what we just did there?
The moment you pin down the butterfly so that you can
carefully study it is the exact moment in which that butterfly
can no longer fly.

It's the motion,
the movement,
the flying,
that makes a butterfly a butterfly.

**Being animates forms,
it doesn't get trapped in them.**

There are lots of names for it,
there needs to be.

This is why when people argue for the existence of God you
sometimes get this feeling that they're actually denying God
in the process.
Exactly.
To try to prove the existence of God is to place God in the
same old forms as everything else when God is the name for
Being Itself.

God is not detached from the world,
up there,
or above,
or somewhere else,
that would make God a form like everything else.

Poetry does such a better job of naming the divine—
you get glimpses,
snapshots,
presence,
lightning bolts,
hints,
signs of where it's headed.

Because if you freeze it,
you've just lost its primary essence.

When we talk about God,
we're not talking about that which
does
or
does not exist,
we're talking about what the nature of
this
is.
This world,
this phenomenon we know to be life,
this event we find ourselves in.

We're not trying to prove anything,
we're naming
this.

God is not a question about what may or may not be
up there
or

above
or
out there—
God is what we're unquestionably
in.
And no one is arguing about that.
We all agree on this
being
that we are all experiencing.

A verb more than a noun,
a direction as much as a beginning.

Which brings us back to us.
What we know about our universe is that it never stops
unfolding. Something bonds with something else and that
produces something new, on and on it goes, for thirteen
billion years
so far.
It's a dynamic reality.
Always changing.
Even our bones are made of atoms, which are swirling,
frenetic relationships of energy.

It took me years to see that the constant flux of my life isn't
a problem, it's a truth about the fundamental nature of this
universe we call home.

I stumbled into what I wanted to do with my life when I was
twenty-one. That first talk in that grove of pine trees at that

camp, it changed everything. It gave my life direction and focus. It was like a rebirth.

And yet working it out, following it where it leads, sorting out how to do that and where to do that and when to do that—it's taken everything I have. It's pinned me to the ground in frustration and despair a number of times. It's been euphoric, exhilarating, exhausting, maddening—that list is long.
Not because something was wrong
but because this is how it works.

It's all part of it.

I notice something happening more and more during this time as I travel and meet people and do more and more events.
It's subtle,
and
really fascinating.

A massive number of people were handed a way of seeing the world that doesn't work anymore. When I was first starting out I saw this disorientation and deconstruction happening here and there. But then, later, I see it everywhere.

I'm in some new space and people are asking questions and I notice how often their question begins with some background.

Before I get to my question I need to tell you about . . .
or
Just to give you a bit of my history . . .

Like that.
Texas, London, Alabama, Toronto, Brazil, Australia, Ohio.
Fresno.
The same thing is in the air everywhere.
A need to let me know that there's a story unfolding here.
It's got history.
They've seen some things,
left some things,
they're rethinking
everything.

I hear sharp and insightful and heartfelt questions about
how to keep going when you've just left a whole way of life,
when nothing seems solid anymore, when you've got way,
way more questions than answers. When the story your
tribe told you isn't big enough to embrace the story that's
unfolding all around you.

At first,
I try to give good answers.
But then,
over time,
I see something else going on,
just below the surface.

A need.

A need to know they're not alone.
To be reassured that there's not something wrong with them.
To have all that disorientation validated.

Listening to them takes me back to that truth about
particles, the one about how observing the motion of a
particle affects what the particle does.

Viewing the particle changes its motion.
Measuring the particle alters what it does.
Seeing the particle effects which course it takes.

This truth reminds me of what happens when a friend is
going through some trauma or loss or injury or betrayal and
you go over to their house. You sit with him, you put your
arm around her, you're present with them in their pain.

And what do they say later?
Thank you, just having you there made all the difference.

But you didn't fix it, did you?
You didn't make it go away,
you didn't get rid of the issue.
Whatever their problem was,
they still had that problem when you left.

What you did was witness it.

And that's what sticks with them,
so much so that they mention it later.

You witnessing their pain affected their experience of their pain.

At some subterranean level of the heart, what we all want is for another human to say,
I see you.

This is one of the great gifts we give each other.

We notice.
We acknowledge.
We see.

That one line—
I see you
—whether spoken or simply experienced,
that one line holds so much,
explains so much . . .

Think of how much violence in our world comes from the hands of those who have never felt seen. When there aren't jobs or education or options or basics like food and water and health care—
and no one seems to care—
of course people get angry.
It becomes political and societal and structural,
but it often starts deeply personal:
No one sees.

The injustice,
the oppression,

the exploitation,
someone was getting away with it—
and those who could stop it didn't see.
Or, they saw,
and they looked away.
Indifferent.

And then, as it always does, the pain escalates in concentric
circles outward, from a question to a longing to a wounded
bitterness to a simmering anger to a bomb to a vote for the
most toxic candidate ever in a desperate attempt to blow the
system up.
All of it often beginning with that initial aching appeal:
Do you see this?
Do you see what I'm going through there?
Do you see me?

I start to see how many of us simply need to know that we're
not alone, that we're not the first, that this
disorientation
and
discovery
and
rethinking of everything
is
normal.

Of course.
I often begin my responses with these two words.
Of course you feel this way.

I watch as I say this.
I watch their body language, I watch as they relax.
Sometimes tears come.
So much pent-up fear and tension,
all those hours and years wondering if there's something
wrong with them.
New forms are needed,
and that usually requires a step into the unknown,
that's often going to have a little fear lurking in it.

Of course you're limping a little.
Of course it can make you feel dizzy.
Of course it's lonely at times.

Spirit moves.
The old forms don't work like they once did.
Of course that's destabilizing.
Of course that can make it hard to tell up from down, left
from right.
Of course it can seem like it was easier back then.

So many have been told by their tribe of origin that
they've lost their way. So many have been told that they're
in dangerous territory, entertaining all these new and
questionable ideas.

I tell them about the word *radical.*
It comes from the Latin word *radix,* which means
root.
A radish is a root vegetable.

The radical is not the person who wandered off the path into
the deep weeds. The radical is the one who went back to the
origins, to the roots, to how it all began.
Sometimes the tribe has lost its way,
sometimes the ones claiming to be the orthodox, correct,
pure ones have gone off the rails,
sometimes it's the mother ship that has lost its bearing,
and it's the radical who's actually rediscovering the true path.

Welcome to the tradition.

I often say this to people.
Welcome to the path people have been walking for
thousands and thousands of years.
I talk about how when we listen for Spirit and then follow
it where it leads into new creation, we're joining with an
untold number of people from across the ages.
That ache, the question, those tentative first steps into
new territory can be lonely. It can also connect us. We're
experiencing what they experienced, we're feeling what they felt.
We're not alone in this, we're joining up with untold masses.
Welcome to the tradition.
I tell people this.
I repeat it to myself, often.
Welcome to the tradition.

There are showers on the beach near where I surf.
I stop and wash the salt water off my board on the way to my
car. Often in the mornings there are people on my right and

left using those showers who spent the night on the beach. They usually have a shopping cart there on the sidewalk next to those showers or a bike loaded down with plastic bags and clothes. Some of them have a dog.

Sometimes we talk,
other times they're in their world,
I'm in mine.

There's a man who sleeps in the alley behind the store at the end of our block. I see him at night when I'm walking our dog. We say hello to each other. He has a bucket of water he uses to clean himself in the morning just before the store opens. And then he disappears. And then I see him later that night.

Around the corner someone has set up a tent next to the UPS Store. There's a vacuum cleaner on the sidewalk next to that tent. There's another tent next to the dollar store a few blocks over that's been set up on a nice rug.

I read the latest estimate that there are sixty thousand people who are without housing in the greater Los Angeles area. I don't know how to begin to process that number.
Sixty thousand.
It's a problem.
It's an emergency.
It's a crisis.
It's lots of things all at the same time.

There are articles in the news every day about it. About
them. There are community groups and nonprofit agencies
and announcements from the mayor's office and new
initiatives related to housing and mental health. There's a
billboard a few blocks over from our house advertising a
new podcast devoted to these issues.

It's overwhelming.
And that number. Sixty thousand.
There's something about that number that speaks to me
about all those billions and billions and billions of atoms
and particles that make
you, *you*
and
me, *me.*

When two particles are bonded and then they separate,
they continue to demonstrate an awareness of each other.
Split two particles, change the spin on the one, and the spin
on the other changes as well. This happens regardless of
the distance between them, without any communication
between the two. They each know what the other is doing,
long after they've parted.

And you and I, that's what we're made of: billions and billions
and billions of these bondings and partings, comings and
goings, getting together and separating, all maintaining an
awareness of each other after they've parted ways.

This is called *entanglement.*

Have you ever been with someone and then hours or days later it feels like you're still carrying that interaction around with you, like they're still with you in some hard-to-define way?

Have you ever had the awareness that way more was going on in the space between you and another person than you could ever describe using words?

Who knows what goes on in the space between us?
Who knows what kinds of exchanges are taking place between us, literally, in our bodies?
Who knows how entangled we are with each other?

This reminds me of that Genesis creation poem, where the poet describes this Spirit energy that's been moving through all of creation, animating and activating all this bonding and uniting. Lots of different traditions throughout history have named this animating energy in lots of different ways. In the early Jesus tradition, they called it
Christ.

They wrote of how through Christ everything came into existence.
They spoke of this same animating Christ energy that forms the sun and the stars forming each one of us.

There is something of the universe in each of us.
They understood this Christ, then, to be both
universal

and
particular.
Both
cosmic
and
personal.

The same Christ,
animating and energizing all of it.
There's a line in the New Testament:
He holds all things together.

All of it.
All of us.
Everybody, everywhere,
in Christ.

This is one of the reasons why the early Jesus movement
grew with such passion and intensity. In a brutally
hierarchal ancient world where massive empires oppressed
and dominated the vulnerable and marginalized—where
everybody knew their place—to announce that there's a
dignity and honor in being human, that every one of us has
infinite worth and value—that was a radical idea.

That was good news.
Still is.

You aren't an object,
you aren't a pawn,

you aren't an accident,
you aren't disposable,
you aren't here to be stepped on,
you aren't here to be exploited for your labor or body or
production value or vote,
you possess Spirit.
Personal, intimate, infinite, knowing, Spirit.
You reflect the divine, present in each of us.
You're *in Christ.*

These early writers used a particular image to describe this
collective unity of humanity, they called us a
body.
The
body
of
Christ.

All of us,
all humans ever,
across time,
all together,
adding up to something.
The body of the Christ.

This is what the universe has been doing the whole time.
And it's very, very mysterious. Because when atoms bond
with atoms, that creates a molecule. A molecule isn't just
a group of atoms, it has properties and characteristics that
aren't present in atoms. Something emerges when you add

atoms together, something more than atoms, something you can't locate within atoms.

Something new.

Like a flock of birds. They fly along and then turn this way, they turn that way. Which bird decides where they fly?
None of the birds do.
When birds fly together, they develop something like a shared mind that doesn't exist in any one of the birds, it only exists when the birds are together.

A bit like 2 + 2 equaling 17.
Same with molecules. Molecules bond with molecules, and that forms cells that have properties that aren't present within molecules.

So when we come together as humans,
something new gets created,
something that isn't present in any one of us.
We form something together.
A body.

Jesus says to his students at one point,
You are in me,
and I am in you.

In another place he says,
I am with you always.

Another time he says,
This is my body.

Yes, of course, a body.
All of us, part of the same body.
This is our body.
All of us entangled.

If a doctor tells you that there is something seriously wrong
with your leg, you would not laugh and say,
Whatever.
You would be alarmed,
and you would seek help,
immediately.
Because what's happening in one part of your
body
inevitably affects the rest of your body because ultimately
you have one
body.

Every part everywhere exists within a whole.
All divisions take place within a unity.

The more I see these people every day all around me,
all of them adding up to sixty thousand, the more
something new begins to happen in me,
something related to this word
them.

I find this word
them

fading as this other word takes its place—
us.

Less
me and them
and more
all of us, together in this.

Yes, this is a problem.
Yes, this is a crisis.
It's also a truth about a body.
Our body.
The body we all form together.

Something about how we have arranged our common life
together isn't working for a growing number of people.
I can see *them* as a problem to be fixed,
I can also see them as messengers sent to bring us all the
truth about ourselves.

Because if it's not working for some people,
then ultimately it's not working for all of us.

When I drive Violet to and from school we see billboards.
Hundreds of billboards.
They're everywhere in Los Angeles.
And most of these billboards are telling me that there's
something I don't have and if I did have it my life would be
so much better.
They speak to me of lack.

I try to block them out.

I have to.

Because if I gave all those billboards any serious attention, it would drive me to madness.

The mind and heart simply can't take that level of bombardment.

Being advertised to like this.

Same with the internet.

Billions of dollars being spent every day to keep your eyes and mine locked on the screen for one. more. click.

This is all new.

No people anywhere have ever lived with this.

In many ways it's like an experiment.

And we're getting the results back.

And what we're learning is that this modern system can easily drive a person crazy.

That word *crazy*.

I notice how many people use it regularly.

How are things going?

Oh, you know, it's crazy.

Yeah, I know what you mean,

it's been crazy lately.

How did this word get normalized?

What is it about the pace of life?

About the noise of life?

About the insanity of modern life that this is a word people regularly use with a straight face to describe what they're experiencing?

My son Trace told me that in one of his classes in college the professor asked the students why they chose their particular majors, and most of them answered, *Because those jobs make the most money.*

We have a problem with the ladders.
They're leaning against the wrong buildings.
Some aren't leaning against anything at all.

We're all entangled,
and these people I see every day,
asking for money,
wandering out into traffic,
sleeping in front of stores and on benches all around my
neighborhood,
they're telling us something about
our body.
About where this is all headed.
About who we're all becoming.
About how this system isn't working for some,
which means it isn't working for all of us . . .

This truth about how we're all connected raises a question about this universe we live in,
the one that's been unfolding and expanding for 13 billion years, constantly producing new life and new forms.

Is the universe done?

At one point, atoms were new.
Then molecules were new, the universe hadn't seen them
before.
And then cells emerged, that was a first.

Is the universe finished, or will it keep going?

And if it keeps going, are there new things that don't
exist now that will come into existence sometime in the
future?
And what would that look like?

Are you and I like cells that make up some larger body?
Is this the new layer that has yet to emerge in the
universe?
Something new the universe hasn't seen before?
What happens when we come together?
Do we all together across the ages form a body?

A nation, a country, a state, a planet—they're all bodies.
If millions of people are hungry or angry, or resentful, or
feel left out and forgotten, that's going to affect the entire
body.
We're all part of the same body.

Obvious,
and
revolutionary.

To discount what *those* people are feeling, or what *they're* going through, or what *they've* been experiencing is to deny and avoid what's present in OUR body.

If it's their problem,
then
it's our problem.

A body can't be against itself.

All that hate on the internet,
racism,
violence,
increasing polarization,
an ever-widening gap between the rich and everybody else—
the list goes on,
all of it grieving and provoking and agitating us because we intuitively know that we are here to come together to make something new the universe has never seen before.

Those different particles there at the beginning all formed one universe.
Same with those atoms,
those molecules—
all the differences and divisions between them took place within a larger
whole.

These are cellular and atomic and molecular truths.
They're also social and political and economic truths.

Your body has all these different parts,
and yet it's all part of your one body.
All that difference takes place within a larger oneness.
You're one, and you're many.
We're one, and we're many.

This is why the division and pain and resentment we see
around us affect us like they do. We intuitively know that this
isn't the path forward because for us to be here, something had
to bond with something like it, over and over and over again.

We feel it in our cells,
because for us to be us,
this is what has been happening in our cells.

It can be excruciating to witness,
and yet nothing is ultimately isolated,
matter is relationships,
all divisions exist within a larger oneness,
and
everything is related to everything else.

Think of the most obnoxious person you know. Someone
who has the supernatural ability to get under your skin.
Picturing them?
Good.
Now, imagine that they're your teacher. That they're here in
your life to teach you something.

I know, it's so hard at first.

It's like a muscle,
it takes a while to build it up.
Let's imagine they're here to show you something,
to teach you how to more fully participate in the wonder
and mystery and vitality of your life.

A few questions:
Why do they annoy you?
What is it about them that gets under your skin?
Can you name it?

Now, is that present anywhere within you?
Are you completely free of it?
Or is there some fear lurking within you that you have this
same whatever-it-is within you?
Is this why they have this unique ability to provoke you like
they do?

Have they come to help you see what you're terrified might be
true about you?
Do they provoke you because they're holding up a mirror to
you, and you don't like what you see?
You are not free in this way,
and the joy is in being free.
What a gift this person is.

Or maybe not.
Maybe it's something awful they do and it's nowhere in you.
More questions:
Why do you care so much?

Lots of people do awful things.
Why this person, and these things?
Does this person ignite these energies within you because
this is something you are here to do something about but you
aren't doing it?
Have they been sent to wake you up to your work in the world?
And there's something holding you back,
some fear,
some hesitation,
some insecurity,
something you haven't faced,
and they're like a giant arrow,
pointing to it,
insisting that you can face whatever it is,
you can go into the heart of it,
there's new life in there.
What a gift this person is.

Or
does this person crank you up because they are free in some
way you aren't free?
You resent them,
because they cut the cord and now they fly,
and you're still tied down?
Is it fear? You don't want to disappoint someone? You
might fail? People might not understand if you step into the
fullness of who you are here to be?
Is this why they agitate you like they do?
What a gift.

Do you see what just happened there?
You started with the parts.
Them. You.
You embraced the differences between you and them.
You didn't skip over them,
or deny them,
or pretend like they weren't there.
Then you went into those parts and differences.
Into the awkwardness, the pain, the conflict.
Instead of walking away from them,
you walked closer.
It's as if you went searching for an invitation in the space
between the two of you. An invitation for you to grow, learn,
expand, become bigger.

**You stopped seeing it all as isolated parts, and you started
seeing it as a whole in which everything is related to
everything else.**
You left behind a world of
labels
and
divisions
and
I'm on this side and they're on that side
and
Who do they think they are?
and
They're the problem!
and

It's because of them we're in this mess!
and
a thousand other things that get said and thought all around
us millions of times a day.

It's so exhausting.
All that clinging and grasping.
So much identity and worth coming from
not being them.

There's winning, and there's losing.
Success, failure.
People you like, people you don't.
Friends, enemies.
Reaching your goal, not reaching your goal.
Being able to pay your bills, not being able to pay your bills.
Life, death.
These categories, these parts, are real.
These are all *part* of what makes life, life.
And yet, there's that word *part.*
They're parts.
One over here, another over there.
The thing you wanted to happen might
happen,
and then over here the possibility that it won't
happen.

Whenever there's
this side,
and

that side,
that outcome
and
this outcome,
there is always something undergirding both of them.

The invitation—
and there's always an invitation—
is to embrace the parts for the parts that they are,
and then see those parts within the whole.
There's
me and them.
And then you keep going and you discover
us.

In the fall of 2017 I write a play. I haven't written a play before.

It's about four mountain climbers who come from four different directions and all arrive at the top of a mountain at the same time. It's an absurd, surreal parable, full of odd characters and even odder twists. I show it to my friend Kristin, who's a theater director, and she says she wants to direct it. We cast the play and then do a series of workshop readings at a theater in my neighborhood. I sit in the audience each night, watching the people around me take it in. It brings me so much joy every time they laugh.

A number of theaters are interested in the play. We send the script out. And then we start getting NOs. People say wonderful things about the play, and then tell us it's not the right fit. Their theater is booked for the next two years. It's not the kind of play they do. They're looking for something else. They do character-driven work, not surrealist parables.

One NO after another.
I love this play and want to see it fully staged.
Another NO.
There's a message at the heart of the play that I believe the world needs now more than ever.
Another NO.

Friends ask me how it's going.
At first, I tell them there's lots of interest, we'll see what happens, it's all so exciting, etc., etc.
But as rejections and passes pile up,
I start telling them the truth.
We're getting lots of rejections.

One day I'm at lunch with some friends, and they ask about it, and I notice that as I tell them we keep hearing NO, I feel a rush of something.
An energy, a passion, a burst.
I tell them the story of the rejections like it's a good story.
Like I believe in this story,
like it's a story worth telling.
I actually enjoy telling them about all these failures.
I say NO with a little force,

like I'm in on the joke.
I laugh about it.

It is, after all, a play.
Everything you need to know is in that word.
Play.
Telling my friends sitting there at lunch that NO story—
something wells up within me.
A defiance.
An energy.
A joy.
Not defeat
but vitality.

**I gradually begin to see that the whole thing is rigged in
favor of our growth.**
The universe has been expanding for thirteen billion
years,
and it never stops inviting us to expand right along with it.
Everything that comes our way, then, is another invitation
to grow.
The YES responses, the NO responses.
The meltdowns, the injustices, the wrongs—
all of it.
Success, failure.
Acceptance, rejection.
There's something lurking in all of it.
An invitation in all of it.
The universe is rigged in favor of our growth.

I think about all the people who have moved me over the years. All those innovators and activists and mentors and voices who stood up for something and got shot at, mocked, rejected, and critiqued.

It did something to them. It made them stronger, more resilient, more committed.

They got so much resistance, but they kept going
is the story we tell about them. All that NO was converted into new life. New commitment. New devotion. New help for others who needed it.

They tapped into some whole,
some truth,
some source,
way beyond all those parts and divisions and YES and NO.

Being Itself.
I AM.
You ground yourself in that,
and you're all of it.
You root yourself in the source and Spirit beyond all these forms and categories and labels, you listen to that and follow that and you keep going.
Result. No result.
Yes. No.
You win. You lose.
You're playing a different game.
You're in it for the life of it.

I'm learning that life is found in all of it.

I keep coming back to that word *play.*
It's a play, Rob.
That should tell you something.
That's what keeps resounding in my head and heart.
It's a play.
All of it.

It's January 2019 and I get an idea for a book.
I've been writing books since 2004. A new one every year or
two. I always have three or four or five ideas and outlines for
books rattling around in my head. A few different times I
finish writing one book and start writing the next book *the*
next day.

And then the well dries up.
I have no idea why.
I haven't written a book in over three years.
I don't have any compelling ideas for a book.
I wonder if I'm done writing books, if that was a chapter and
now it's over.

But then I get this idea.
It comes very quickly.
I can't type fast enough.
It's a frenetic explosion of ideas and insights and
connections, looping back on itself and then surging
forward. There's a story about the Vans store in California

I went to as a kid. A section on how observing the particle affects what it does. It's all over the place.

I want it to feel less like a read and more like a ride, like you'd been caught up in an extended riff about life and death and art and science that shows you how astonishing it is to be alive in such a way that it leaves you breathless and intoxicated in the end.

Out it comes, that first draft,
like an explosion.
Page after page.
Day after day.

I keep coming back to this truth that everything is connected to everything else, the whole thing an endless invitation to participate . . .

I'm so happy because it's been years since I've done this and this one is coming with such flow. One big idea after the next—

But it's missing something.
I don't know what.
The ideas are there,
and the writing feels fresh,
like I'm walking this thin line between frenetic and focused,
just what I think the book needs.
But it's still missing something.
I can't figure out what.

I sit with it for days, weeks, trying to figure it out.
Some days I sit for hours and type nothing.
No progress.
Other days I type and type,
and then at the end of the day I delete everything I wrote.

And then, out of nowhere, I remember how my grandma
used to keep cash in her bra.
I haven't thought about that in years.
Where did that come from?
Should I tell that story in the book?
Yes, I think.
But where? What does that have to do with any of this?
I have no idea.
I wonder,
What if I started the book with it?
The idea is so absurd I try it.
Oh, that's interesting.
I picture her and me sitting on that porch of hers, sometimes
talking, sometimes not talking, sometimes just sitting there
listening to the wind.

I feel this strange tenderness in my heart,
like I'm back there on that porch,
in between being a boy and a man.
This new space opens up within me.
I remember how she would talk about Preston.
Out comes a bit about Preston.
Then I write about Douglas.
And then my dad.

I type up that part about him finding out that his dad had
died in the car on the way to the funeral.

I can feel tears just below the surface.
I keep telling the story,
how I picked up on that loss from a young age.
I hadn't seen it like that before.
Is that what that was?
Suddenly, a whole bit of my history makes a little more
sense.
I start to cry, sitting there writing all that.
I've spent a lot of time over the years scouring my insides,
searching through my history,
but this, this is new.

I come back the next day,
and I keep going.
More story,
more tears.

The ache is so sharp,
it pierces me,
and yet there's so much energy there.
Like I can't keep the words in.

Eileen, Preston, my dad, his brother, my son Trace, my son
Preston. Violet.
Like a raw nerve pulsing.
Out it comes.

Where is this coming from?
I find myself asking.
Why is this story melting me like this?
It makes me feel small.
Like a kid.

I wanted this book to be a big book of even bigger ideas. The biggest ideas imaginable.
I wanted this book to blow your mind,
showing you your life and the universe in a whole new way.

But now,
I'm writing about my grandma.

And even more unexpectedly,
this is where all the power is for me.
This feels huge, like all those big ideas fit just fine right next to all that loss and ache and possibility.

I find myself asking,
Where did those big ideas come from?
followed by,
When did I first come across them?
followed by,
What was it like when all these ideas were new to me?
followed by,
How did I come to see the world the way I do?
followed by,
How did I get here?

I find myself wondering what that book would be like, a book where I traced where those ideas came from back to when it was all new.

A book about what happened,
and what it did to me.

Which takes me back to the farm. And the cabin. And soil and sand and water and that sense that there's more going on here.

One Saturday Kristen and I are with our friend Sheryl. The last time we'd seen Sheryl she'd come to a show I'd done in Brooklyn. Sheryl's an actor and director, and she tells me how she experienced my show. She has so much wisdom about the dynamics of performing and shows, I'm like a sponge around her. Sheryl has this universal mother earth strength and grounding that swallows you up—it's a ruthless authenticity that makes you feel so loved and valued that you want the unvarnished truth. You want her to tell it to you like it truly is. Somewhere in the course of our conversation I mention how I'd paced the show so it would gradually make more and more sense and then hopefully at the end there'd be this big *AHA!!*
moment and it would all come together.
I use the word *payoff,* as in
And then at the end there's this big payoff.
She stops me.
She disagrees.
No, Rob Bell, she says.

She then launches into this explanation about how she
doesn't come to my show because I know something she
doesn't and if she sits there long enough I'll reveal it to her.
She says she comes because
We all get to discover it with you.
This floors me.
And then she says,
It's all payoff, Rob Bell.

I'm so overwhelmed it takes me a bit to collect myself.
It's all payoff.

You know that feeling when an elevator drops unexpectedly
just an inch or so and you feel that whoosh in your body?
That's what it felt like when she said that. In my heart.
It's all payoff.

In that moment I see something I haven't seen before.
A trap.
A trap to being Rob Bell.

I'm transported back,
way back,
across the years,
to all those hours of studying and learning and inhaling
information and thinking and reflecting about all these big
ideas about grace and love and Spirit. That was all good.
And necessary. But ever so gradually it worked a sort of spell
on me. I know some things. I'd love to tell you them. I'd love
to show you. I'd be happy to teach you.

I see what that can do over time.
It can separate.
Me *here*, others *there*.
Me talking, others listening.
Me writing, others reading.

And that's true,
in one sense.
There are parts.
We each have our role to play,
our gift to give.
But there are also wholes.
I'm me, yes.
and I'm also everybody.

When I look far enough inside of you, I'll
find me.
When I look far enough inside me, I'll find you.

I locate something deeper within me.
An impulse, a posture.
It has a spatial dimension to it.
I'm laughing, and winking, and smiling, and welcoming
everybody.
But oh so subtly it's me *here*,
and others *there*.

Hang in there, everybody, the payoff is coming.
I'm about to show it to you . . .

But Sheryl, Sheryl says,
It's all payoff.
She doesn't come because I'm here and she's there,
she comes because we're all here in the same place
discovering together.

**Later that summer I'm in San Francisco for a stop on my
speaking tour. I'm sitting on a stool, taking questions from
people who have come two hours early for a preshow Q&A.**
People can ask anything they want.
I love it.
I learn so much.

We're not far into it when a woman in the front row asks a
question. She tells me that her husband recently committed
suicide and she's struggling with how a person can believe
there is any ultimate goodness in the world when something
like that happens. She asks about suffering and God and loss
and believing and not believing and how to keep going after
what she's been through.

I can feel everybody lean in.
The air shifts a bit.
No one moves.

I pause.
I put my hand on my heart.
I've been doing this a lot lately, putting my hand on my

heart before I speak. This gesture reminds me to stay here, in my heart, in my body.

An earlier me would have charged in at this point with words. I come from a particular intellectual tradition that placed a great priority on the mind.
Analyze.
List.
Define.
Give some practical steps.

As she's asking her question my mind does what it's been doing for years, racing through
answers
and
information
and
well-formed paragraphs
and
stories
and
examples.

I can do this all day.

But there's a trap in all that.
It separates.
Me here,
her there.
Her asking the questions,

me being the answer man.

That's not what I'm after, separation.
I'm after something else . . .

I keep my hand on my heart.
No, not yet.
Don't speak.
Listen.
Join her.
The story is the truth,
the mystery is born in bodies.
It's all payoff.
I get the setup. I'm aware that these people have paid
more money for a premium ticket and a better seat so
they can come to a Q&A with Rob Bell before the show
and ask questions and I'll give answers. I'm fine with
that. If that's the door that we all came through,
that's fine.

It's a form,
and there's nothing wrong with the form.
It brought us here,
together.

But that's just a starting point.
A premise.
A setup.
A door to another room.
If we start with me *here,*

and her *there,*
fine.
But what's compelling to me,
what moves me and opens my heart up,
is to start here and then follow it wherever it goes.
Not control,
listening.
Following.
Presence.
I'm looking for that moment when the boundaries dissolve
in some new way and it's us,
together,
going somewhere new.

That moment when I find me in you,
and you find yourself in me.

Let's walk together.

I ask her if she's grieving two deaths.
Her husband. And her God.
She nods.
They both died.
Yes, she says,
That's what's happened.

Because that's often what happens. We have a whole world
constructed and then we experience a trauma in which we
lose way more than we first realized.

I ask her if the God who doesn't let husbands kill themselves
died when her husband died.
Yes, she says.

The room shifts, just a bit.
We're moving, I can subtly feel it.
When she first asked her question I was aware of the room—
I've felt this a thousand times, felt people wondering,
How is Rob going to answer this?

Not a lot of people want to sit on a stool and answer
questions about suicide.

But now we're slowly gliding past that setup,
that setup in which I'm the answer man,
here to take your difficult questions.

We're merging, just a bit.
moving past that form that got us here . . .

I tell her about my own experiences of God dying. How
Jesus on the cross saying,
My God, my God, why have you forsaken me?
is the day God becomes an atheist.

She smiles for the first time.
I tell her what I've learned about how some gods have to die.
They help for a while, they give structure and meaning and
some order, until they don't.

I ask her about this.
She has a lot to say.
I learn from her.

There's a back-and-forth starting to emerge here.
Her story.
My story.
The people sitting around us.
The mystery born in bodies.

I put my hand back on my heart.
Don't race ahead, I tell myself.
Don't fix it, because you can't fix this.
This pain, ache, her loss.
Don't think the mind can resolve this, it can't.
Slow down.
Stay here.
Everything you need is right here,
I remind myself.

I have these old impulses, shaped from years of trying to
help people. Urges to race ahead and give the answer,
to tell everybody that it's all going to be fine, to stay a step
ahead of the pain with ideas and truth and insights and
hope. Just be funny, keep moving, just keep talking, just do
something so we don't have to sit in it and feel it fully. These
impulses go way, way back in me.

I can feel them fading.
They just don't have the power they used to.

Listen.
That's what I hear.
Listen.
I ask her if I can give her an image that has helped me.
She nods.
In that ancient Genesis poem, the one that begins the
Bible, it all begins with chaos, formless void, and darkness
hovering over the waters. In ancient Hebrew consciousness,
water is the unknown. The depths. The abyss.

And in the poem,
Spirit is hovering over those waters.
That word *hover* there is the same image as a bird flapping
its wings, hovering . . .
And then Spirit enters into those waters and out of them
creates something new. Something vast and expansive and
beautiful and diverse.

God, I love that image.
The poet describes all the beauty and goodness and design
of this world as coming out of chaos and formless abyss.

We know those waters.
Loss and pain and grief and wounds and not knowing what
to do or where to go or how to deal with the agony of life.
We know those waters.
There's Spirit in there, hovering, waiting to bring something
new out of it. This is why the people who inspire us the
most
always

have been through those waters.
They've experienced that hovering.
They've seen that new creation.
She knows what I'm talking about, she tells me.

Back and forth we go,
like a dance.
Grief, loss, feeling the full weight of all that pain.
She says that she's already noticed new and unexpected life
coming out of this abyss she's been in, out of those waters
she's been drowning in.

I don't know how long this exchange takes place.
Her initial question.
My question back to her.
Three minutes?
Ten?
Twenty?
Time is bendy.
I lose track of it.
So do the people around me.
We've all been somewhere, together.
We're still there,
sitting in that theater,
participating in that ROB BELL preshow Q&A,
and yet we've been all over the place.
In our histories, our memories, our stories.
We've covered a lot of ground,
sitting there in those chairs.

I'm still thinking about her question,
days later.
This happens all the time,
I meet people,
we have an exchange,
they tell me about their lives,
they bring their questions,
I bring mine.
I think of the story of Jesus showing his student Thomas his
crucifixion wounds after his resurrection, essentially saying
to Thomas,
Even these belong.

That's new creation.
New creation includes all of it,
all that came before.
That's what happens when you own it all.
You enter into those waters,
discovering in the process a whole new world coming into
being, a new world that includes all that came before it.

There's a mystery here, how the universe could be such an
expansive place that the events we initially experience as
heartbreaking
and
tragic
and
wrong
could, given enough time,

open us up
and make us
bigger
and
more loving
and
more grounded
people.

Which is why those first Jesus followers used to explain this great mystery by telling the story of Jesus being executed on a cross.

He doesn't explain the suffering—
as if the evil people do to each other could be explained
—he *bears* it.
He takes it into the expanse of his being.

And not passively, like he has no other options.
Actively, willfully—like he's tuned in to some great secret involving a wholeness that all the parts ultimately belong to.

Once again, the poetry of it.
The story isn't over,
it's just beginning.
They kill him,
but it isn't the last word.
It's the first word of a new world.
Violence doesn't have the last word,
love does.

The suffering doesn't end the story,
it unleashes a whole new story . . .

No wonder people still wear crosses,
thousands of years later.
This sign, this symbol speaks to that question we've all
asked:
Can something new be created out of even this?

That's the question lurking there in all our dark waters,
that's the invitation that never stops coming our way,
to see the whole of it,
to grow bigger,
to expand along with the universe.
To learn all over again that our bodies can include
even this.

This moment,
this pain,
this loss,
this fear,
this encounter—
is Spirit hovering over
even these waters?

That annoying neighbor,
chronic pain,
toxic relatives,
debt,
the threat of physical violence,

petty coworkers,
children who continually break your heart,
a lover who just left,
another school shooting . . .
Can something new be created out of even this?

Yes.
Spirit's in all of it.
In *everything.*
In all those dark waters,
hovering.

Years ago I spoke at an event in Chicago that was put on by *Time* magazine.
Actually, I was on a panel.
The last panel I've ever been on.
I can't stand being on panels.
I will gladly sit in the audience and enjoy listening to whoever it is talk about whatever their thing is. Or I will gladly take the mic and do my thing.
But panels, no way.
Torture for me.
Just can't do them.
Sitting there, waiting your turn.
Not wanting to take up too much time,
but wanting to say *something.*

At the beginning of that panel discussion, we were asked to introduce ourselves and give a brief description of what we

do. The other people on the panel, they were so clear and
concise. One man was helping people get access to clean
water, one woman was helping educate Muslim women.
So impressive.
And articulate.
I stumbled through my answer.
And that's being generous.
I made no sense.
Like I probably shouldn't be on a panel.
I beat myself up over that answer for months.
Have I come this far, worked this hard, to not even be able to
give a brief description of what I do with my life?

I was afraid to own up to what I do.
Because it sounds so . . .
Woo-woo?
That might be the word.
Vague?
There's that as well.

I'm filled with more wonder and awe than ever,
and I want everybody everywhere to have more wonder and
awe.

I want everybody to say YES to that invitation.
We have plenty when we're kids.
A bug on the sidewalk has us enthralled.
We get a new bike and we ride for hours. Days.

So yes to the ancient wisdom tradition,

yes to everything is spiritual,
yes to new readings of the Bible,
yes to the Jesus tradition,
yes to the truths found in every tradition everywhere,
yes to science and art and waves and stories,
yes to shows and books and events and plays—
but underneath it all,
what I'm after is the wonder and awe.

I want to help people rediscover the wonder and awe of their
existence.

I shied away from saying this for years because,
well, *say that on a panel.*

So I tried to fit in,
but that didn't work.
If I were on that panel again—
I'd probably say,
*Hi, I'm Rob. And I love helping people rediscover the wonder
and awe of their lives, because that's the starting point. That's
where we begin, that's what we all want . . .*

See, it's a little vague and over the top,
and yet it's great, isn't it?
Of course I could go on about being a spiritual teacher
rooted in the ancient Jesus movement . . .

And if after hearing that someone from the audience
shouted,

Enough with the panel! Tell us more!
That would be weird, but I'd be happy to say more.
I'd start with your parents.

Because in the beginning, your parents had sex.
That's how you got here.
In *your* beginning, your mother and father got together and
somewhere in the course of that encounter your father made
his—let's call it his
contribution—
of roughly 250 million sperm of which
one
eventually made it to your mother's egg, fertilized that egg,
and that egg eventually became
you.

Those are terrible odds,
and that's a massive amount of inefficient waste,
and yet
here
you
are.

The rest of those sperm didn't make it.
The scientific terminology for this is:
They died.

Your parents had sex,
and millions and millions of sperm died,
and one didn't.

That's millions and millions of deaths and failures
and unmet potentials. All that death, right there in
your beginning, woven into your origins, brushing up
against all that explosive creative potency that eventually
became you.

We know we're going to die,
we know this is where we're all headed
in the end,
but death was also there
in your beginning.

Sometimes people talk about death as if it's the thing that
comes after this.
There's life,
which we're in now,
and then death,
which we'll be in when this life is over.

**But death, death doesn't enter abruptly when life is over,
death is present in all of creation every step of the way.**
All of your creation.

All around us all the time,
life and death are in close proximity,
all of it totally *natural.*

Those lines are blurred,
these two have been dancing together your entire life.

And before that.

Of course we feel close to those who have died.
Of course we meet people and we say,
I feel like I've always known you.
Of course people for thousands of years have talked about
communicating with those who have come and gone ahead
of us.
Of course some people insist this isn't their first go-around.

The borders and boundaries are way, way more porous than
we could ever imagine. There's a great line from the Bible
about how
we're surrounded by a great cloud of witnesses.
Yes. Of course.
Where else would they be, all those who have come
before us?

Sometimes people are adamant that this life is all
there is and then it's over permanently. Finally. Forever.
That's it.
But how small and impoverished would a person's intellect
and imagination have to be to confidently and definitively
declare that
this—
this narrow span of years,
this brief experience in these bodies,
this fleeting glimpse of space-time here on this planet
—is all there is?

Think about all of the extraordinary things we've learned
from science and how the more we discover, the more we
see how much we don't know. Has there ever been any
scientist anywhere who's ever announced that there's
less than we'd thought?
Less mystery?
Less to explore?
Less we don't know?

No. It's always more. Every time.
We only ever learn that there's more out there,
in here, around us.
Of course.
We've only ever just been getting started.

Which brings us back to death.
There is death
at the end of life,
but for you to be here
there was death, lots of it, millions and millions of times over,
at the start of your life.

We don't know what happens when we die.
That's true.
But no one knew what was going to happen when you were
born either.
Who you would become.
How your life would go.
What you would do.
What would happen to you.

There's a mystery about what you'll experience at the end of
your life,
and there was a world of mystery there at the beginning of
your life.

This is why new parents spend hours and hours sitting by
that crib, staring at their new baby.
What have we created here?
Who is this person?
What is this life going to become?

The questions are intoxicating.
You can think of little else.
What a teacher,
those new babies,
showing us what kind of universe we're living in.

Somewhere around 250 million of your father's
contribution
died
in the creation of you.
That's a lot of deaths.

So who knows if your death at the end of your life isn't
another beginning much like all those deaths were?

Because ends always generate beginnings.

Speaking of your beginning, only 20% of sperm have what's
considered a decent shape—some have two heads, 90% were

dead within the first half hour, and at first your mother's
body thought your father's contribution were
intruders.

Her immune system went on high alert because of how
foreign your father's contribution appeared and then tried to
kill them with deadly acid.

To be clear, the part of you that comes from your father
*your mother's body tried to exterminate in their first
encounter.*

The complexity is staggering.
Your mother's body has systems in place to identify possible
threats to her health, and these systems are extremely
efficient in their ability to destroy these threats. But within
these efficient systems are also the capacities to identify
when the first assessment was incorrect and the perceived
threat was actually
an emissary of new life.

Your life has gotten rather complex over time, right?
Bills, stresses, relationships, trying to figure out what you're
here to do, trying to raise a kid, understand yourself better,
do the right thing in sticky situations.
Your life was complicated long before you got here.
You were swimming in complexity and mistaken
assessments and ambiguity from the beginning.
Literally.

Having survived that near extermination, the sperm then had to travel. If your father's contribution was scaled up to the size of a human, it had to reach a destination two hundred miles away. Quickly.

Right away it had to travel through the cervix, which has endless channels that don't go anywhere, like climbing a ladder several miles high only to discover that the ladder isn't leaning against anything. At which point it's too late to turn around and climb down and then climb up another ladder only to learn that that one—you get the point. About 99% of sperm never get past the cervix.

Then the uterus, which is like a vast open plain. At human scale it's roughly two miles long and a half mile wide, and the sperm needs to find one particular opening, which is about two heads wide. At this point about one thousand sperm are dying with every heartbeat.

And then the sperm meet the leukocytes for the first time. The leukocytes sound a bit like the name of an obscure religious sect—but we're not talking about sects—they're white blood cells that protect the mother's body by hunting foreign invaders. They move in gangs and they're larger than sperm and when these cells hunt sperm down they *decapitate*
them.

So there's that.

And then, eventually, if the sperm survives—although we're talking about
you
so the sperm did survive—it arrived at the fallopian tubes
where to gain entry it had to display what can best be
described as *proper swimming ability.*

Like an audition.
Or interviewing for a job.

Your mother's body had to determine if your father's
contribution *had the right moves.*

I know.
I'm thinking the same thing.
We're simply describing the facts of a known and verified
process that happens all the time all around the world
and has been going on for tens of thousands of years and yet
it's almost impossible to not read it at some other level.

Cells and cervixes and movement and attrition and systems
designed to protect and preserve and then somewhere
in your mother's body there was a biological/chemical/
physiological process that assessed your father's sperm's
movement—
that evaluated whether it was good enough
whether it passed,
whether it measured up—
there's something about describing that particular process that
weirdly sounds like, well, your mother and father. *Humans.*

She *did* assess his movements at some point, didn't she? Not just cells and chemicals but . . . what? . . . Hearts? Souls? Minds? Personalities? Character? Compatibility?

And then, at the end, after all that
travel and all those
acids and
gangs and
distances and against all those
odds the sperm gets near her
egg.

A bit about that egg. Your mother started with somewhere between one million and two million eggs. By the time she and your father got together she had around one thousand. And that one egg was going to appear for those few days in the month—

We need to stop there and note for the record that her monthly egg-releasing cycle was influenced—like every woman everywhere since forever—according to the sequential, unflappably consistent movements of the . . . *moon.*

The *moon.*
I'll type that again out of sheer admiration for the unexpected oddness of this particular relationship:
the *moon.*

To be clear, the female body has an intuitive synchronistic

alignment with a rock floating in space 238,000 miles
away.

She's a woman, a human being, right here among us in flesh
and blood, and there's also something about her that is
planetary.

Take a moment,
and put your hand on your heart.
You feel this,
this body you have?
You have a body,
you come from a body,
a body that has a connection with a celestial body hundreds
of thousands of miles away.
There is something universal about us,
something as big as the solar system present within us.

When you can't be at an event that you wish you could
be at,
sometimes you tell the people who will be there,
I'll be with you in spirit.
What do you mean by that?
You won't be there,
but you will?
And yet we all know exactly what you mean.
Sometimes someone we love dies,
and the next time we're at a place that we used to be at with
them,
we can sense them with us.

Like they've left,
but they're still there.
Of course.
They're with us *in spirit*.

This body you have,
the one that you have your hand on right now,

**your body is something that is happening within
you.**

Sometimes people talk about the body as the exterior
boundary of the self. You have a body, and then within
your body may or may not be a Spirit or soul or ghost in
the machine or whatever, depending on your view of these
things.

But you possess Spirit,
and Spirit extends way, way beyond the body.
Your body is something happening within the far larger
phenomenon known as you.

And central to this phenomenon of having a body is our
inherent connection with the sun, moon, and stars.
The connections,
they're endless.

Back to earth, to that one particular egg. It appeared in that
narrow window during that one month, but it didn't go
away. It stayed, and when it sensed that the sperm was near,

it sent out a signal to the sperm that helped the sperm swim
that last bit of distance by boosting it into what is known as
a *hypermotile state.*

I love that. Something within her helped something that
came out of him to achieve *a hypermotile state.*

Her system is highly calibrated to protect her from invaders.
She has a number of processes that can be immediately
instigated to
spray something with deadly acid
or
chop off its head.

You know, lethal.

She is fierce
and
protective
and
strong.

But then this one little fella—
that seems like the right word here, doesn't it?
—this one little fella survives, he endures, he just keeps
going while his . . .
once again, let's find a word . . .
while his
colleagues?

mates?
fellow *seamen*?

Seamen. That's it.

He just keeps going while the ones he started with
are dropping out left and right. Over two hundred
million down, dead, lost—and yet this one little fella
keeps going.

He goes and goes until there's this moment when he's close
enough to the egg that the egg senses his closeness—

Wait.
What?
The egg *senses* his closeness?

Yes, senses.
The egg is . . . aware?
The egg . . . knows?

Yes, exactly.
The egg senses he's close *and helps him.*

Let's stop and enjoy that for a bit. There's a moment when
he's gotten far enough, his endurance and resilience and
indomitable onwardness—
I am so fond of that phrase I'm going to repeat it and bold
it: There is a moment when his **indomitable onwardness**
has gotten him to the point where she no longer treats him

as an invader but those very systems that were previously
calibrated to take off his head
switch
and now these systems through chemical signals and careful
guidance work to bring him to his destination.

In the end, the one she hasn't killed or confused or worn
out or blasted with deadly acid or ignored through sheer
indifference to the insurmountable odds he's facing—
that one
she helps finish his journey.

Like she was ready for this one.

All this happened to make you,
you?
That little fella struggled,
mightily,
and overcame the odds.
That already happened,
for you to be you.

Is this why stories of people overcoming great odds move
and inspire us?
Is this why stories of compassion, caring for each other,
looking out for the vulnerable, stir us so much?
Because this has been happening since our beginning, in
our beginning. It's built into the fabric of creation.

These two energies—

that indomitable onwardness energy that just keeps going
regardless of the odds,
and that listening, sensing energy that takes care of the one
in danger—
these two energies were inextricably intertwined,
working together,
in harmony,
for each of us to be created.

These energies are cosmic,
they're archetypal,
they're sacred,
they're the yin and yang of creation.
They bring it into being,
hold it all together,
keep it balanced.
We've been writing about and singing about and discussing
and noticing the dynamic interplay between these two
energies for thousands and thousands of years.
And for you to be you,
they met and embraced?

No wonder you sometimes have big dreams for your
life.
No wonder you lie awake at night with huge questions.
No wonder you sometimes feel like your heart is going to
burst with the fullness and depth of life . . .
before you were even born the most primordial creative
energies of the universe were coming together to bring you
into existence.

Let's pause here, because something happened a few pages back that we should note. We were humming along there following the reproductive process—that phrase takes a bit of the sexy out of it, doesn't it?

The reproductive process.

It's just so technical, so dry, so lifeless—even though that's the phrase we use to describe this utterly astonishing phenomenon of a human being created.

Which is my point.
I was using rather straightforward terminology from biology like
sperm and
egg and
motility
to describe this process as accurately as possible.
And I could have turned up the knobs a bit, using words like
chromosomes and
pheromones and
amoeboid cells and
macrophages, and I could have even mentioned the *ampulla.*

And with more terminology and more description we would have had more and more detail and information about how we each became us.

But then a few pages back I started referring to your father's
contribution as a *little fella*. And regarding your mother's
responses to his efforts I added a
her
and a
she.

In referring to the sperm as a little fella, that *is* accurate—one
sperm measures 0.05 of a millimeter. (The smallest thing you
can see with your unaided eye is 0.1 mm.) So yes, *little.*
But *fella*?
Sperm don't have gender, they're cells.
And yet we went with it.
Her and *she* and *his* and little *fella.*
And what that did is made it feel a bit more like a story: His
journey and her strength and the obstacles he faced and the
help she gives aren't technically how you'd describe it, and
yet at another level, in another sphere,
we know this story.

These aren't competing descriptions,
they complement each other.
They dance together.

This is one of the great gifts of science—taking things apart,
breaking them down to their smallest components, showing
us with precision and detail how it all works.

And this is one of the great gifts of art—putting things

together that you wouldn't have thought to connect. It's just a sperm cell and an egg, but you start talking about them like it's a man and a woman and it's absurd and strange and yet it resonates somewhere within you—you find yourself thinking,
Keep going, I want to see how this one ends . . .

Back to your father's hypermotile contribution, which reached your mother's eggish embrace and that union formed a zygote.
And then—
you know what happened,
you were there
—that zygote grew.
For nine months.

One month in your heart was forming,
Two months in your bones and face were taking shape,
Three months in you had arms and feet and organs,
Four months in your nervous system was up and running,
Five months in you developed muscles and started growing hair,
Six months in you could hiccup,
Seven months in you could hear sounds and respond to light,
Eight months in you could see while your brain took huge developmental leaps forward,
and by
nine months you could blink and your lungs were working.

In nine months a fetus smaller than a grain of rice became a
human being with all these systems and organs fully integrated
with fingers and toes and a brain and the ability to hiccup.

From
that
to
you?

That's an astonishing increase in complexity.

Within every mother there is a massive increase in intricacy,
from a few cells to the most complicated single living entity
in the universe—and it happens in nine months?

And this happens all the time?
In every mother everywhere?
It's not an aberration, or a one-off, it's how we all became *we
all*?
This has happened billions and billions of times over?
And it keeps happening?
Year after year after year?

If I had never heard any of this and you told it to me,
I don't know if I'd even believe you.
What an astonishing story.
And this story you'd be telling me,
you'd be telling me about the universe and biology
and cosmology and planets and every human being
everywhere,

but you'd also be telling me about
you.

And me.

Sometimes people talk about miracles as if some believe in
them and some don't.
As if the world is humming along,
and then something happened that interrupted that normal,
everyday humming-alongness,
something that broke the rules,
something with no precedent,
and then things went back to their normal ways.

Like there was a break in the routine,
before things returned back to the routine.

I don't believe in miracles like that because the whole thing
is miraculous.
You. Me. All of it.
Is there any precedent for any of it?
There was a bang,
and then thirteen billion years of expansion?
And central to this expansion is the bonding between
similar entities—atoms, molecules, cells—to bring about
new forms?
What?
And this keeps happening,
year after year after year?

The universe keeps going,
keeps creating,
keeps unfolding?

The technical term for all of this is, of course,
miraculous.

And the struggle of it?
Our very conception was steeped in struggle.
She almost exterminated him.
Millions and millions of *hims* didn't make it.
This thing—you—was doomed from the start.
And yet it wasn't.
Because you're here.
Those insanely insurmountable odds were, well,
surmounted.
You've got a dream?
You're trying to change a system that is deeply entrenched
and it doesn't look like you'll be able to change anything?
You're trying to help someone and it feels like all the odds
are stacked against you?
You've been here before.
Struggle is nothing new.
It's baked into all of it.

Which can be really discouraging.
Or you can read back through these past few pages.
Because I was just describing the journey of a sperm in the
fallopian tubes, but you were into it, weren't you?

The struggle, the odds, her taking off the heads of a number
of his comrades,
that's what made it such a great story,
right?

The struggle is what makes it so compelling. We've known
this for thousands of years. The Bible begins with a story
about a people called Israel, and *Israel* essentially means
the one who struggles with God.
I like that.
It rings true.
Struggle is baked into the whole thing.
Which is the invitation for all of us.
To start there.
Of course it's going to be difficult.
What else would it be?
The odds were stacked against us from the get-go.

And yet you're here.
You are the answer to the odds.
And no one is doubting that you're here.
Welcome to the struggle.

You're here because your mother and father came together,
which is what the whole thing has been doing the entire
time. And when they came together, it was probably—
ideally—because of love.
Love brought them together.
Love brought you here.
That's what we call it when humans come together.

What, then, do we call it when particles and atoms and molecules come together?

If we call it *love* when it happens at later stages with more complex forms like your mom and dad and you and me, should we call it *love* when it happens earlier in its less complex forms like atoms and molecules?

Is it all because of love?
All this being,
all this becoming,
all this endless unfolding that keeps creating new layers and forms the universe has never seen before,
is *love* the proper word for all of it?

When we talk about how in the end all that matters are the ones you love,
and we sing that all we need is love,
are we affirming what every atom and cell has been doing the entire time?

And if God is the name for Being Itself,
and love is what it's been doing this whole time,
then
God is love
is a good way to describe this experience we're having,
isn't it?

It's August of 2019 and I'm standing in a field in Denmark, looking out over that field to the ocean.

Next to me is the house that my grandfather Neil grew up in. Neil used to stand in this field, looking out over that ocean, longing for a better life somewhere else.

On my phone I have a picture of him in front of this house in 1903.

I've heard about this house my entire life. Neil's five brothers. His harsh father. The endless work in the fields to survive. His parents rented him out to a local wealthy family, who tied a rope around his waist and lowered him into their sewer to shovel the human waste.

And then, at nineteen, he leaves.
He walks up that dirt road, which is still a dirt road, and he never returns. Never sees his parents again, never sees the home he grew up in.

After years of staring out over that field to the ocean,
he gets on a ship and sails across that ocean,
making it all the way to Los Angeles,
where he starts with nothing.
He builds a business,
he starts a family,
he makes it.

I turn around and take a picture of Violet, who's taking a picture of the house.
She is totally into this.
The details, the stories, the search for this house.

Neil.
I have so many questions.

I bend down and touch the soil.
I'm trembling a bit.
I look out again over the field at the ocean.
I look back up that narrow dirt road that leads toward
town, thinking of him walking that road one last time, not
knowing he'd never come back.

These are my roots,
this story a part of my story,
it's all connected.
I'm somewhere in all of this.

I've come here from Los Angeles,
One hundred years later,
to see it and feel it,
searching for something.
Another bit of who I am?
Another bit of who we are?

You've got your own Neils.
Your own fields.
Your own leaving into the unknown.
We all do.
It's all a part of it.

Why am I in this field?
I'm going back,

which is going forward.
That's how it works.
We come from bodies and places and events,
and we go back there from time to time,
finding pieces of ourselves we didn't know were
there,
because everything is connected to everything
else,
and the more we know about who and where we come
from,
the more we know about where we're headed.

Something brought me to this piece of land at
this time,
something that's a part of me becoming me,
and when I reach down and touch the earth,
there's something infinite there in that soil.

Do you see it?
Do you see what we get to experience?
Put your hand on your heart.
Can you feel it?
Everything is spiritual.
There's a universe there in your chest,
a cosmos in your heart.
We know there's more,
We've known it the entire time.
What a gift.
All that wonder and awe.

I feel like I'm just getting started.
I can't imagine where it's going next.
It's like an endless invitation.
And we get to say yes.
Again and again and again.

ACKNOWLEDGMENTS

A Thousand Thanks to . . .

Chris Ferebee. Nineteen years in and we're just getting started.

Jennifer Enderlin. I'm so grateful for your editing, energy, and helping me not break the spell.

Stratton Robert Glaze. For all those long talks on all those long tour drives and of course that bit from Justo González that helped me see what I've been doing the whole time.

The band MOGWAI for your song "Ether." That song moves me. I listened to it on endless repeat while writing his book.

Jill Rowe. Remember when you and me and Preston drove from London to Bristol for that gig and then back to London later that night and I read an early draft of this book to you out loud from the passenger seat the whole way there and back? That was the best.

Andrew Morgan, Phil Wood, Helen Mom Bell, Ruth Bell Olsson, Chris York, Liz Gilbert, Sheryl Moller, and Kristin Hanggi for reading early drafts and giving me so much love and insight and feedback.

Kristen Bell. This is the part at the very end of the book where I try to fit on a line or two in the THANKS SECTION a bit about how much you had to do with this book. Where do I even begin? There were so many times when I was writing along and I'd type that first-person pronoun *I*, and then I'd stop and think that the more accurate pronoun is *we*. Because you've been here, the whole way, usually a step ahead. So yes, it's my book, but it's our life. And your contribution? All those ideas and all your energy and all your indomitable onwardness and your editing and insistence that it could be even better—let alone your fearlessness and strength and desire to keep going, no matter where it takes us—how could I ever fit that in a few lines at the end of a book?